INTRODUCING ASIAN
FEMINIST THEOLOGY

INTRODUCING

ASIAN FEMINIST THEOLOGY

Kwok Pui-lan

INTRODUCTIONS IN
FEMINIST THEOLOGY

EDITORIAL COMMITTEE

Mary Grey • Lisa Isherwood

Catherine Norris • Janet Wootton

The Pilgrim Press

Cleveland, Ohio

Acknowledgments

Extract from 'Magdalene Dancing in Crimson: A Biblical Noh Drama', *Japan Christian Activity News* (Spring/Summer 1996). Reprinted with permission.

'Set Free' by Dulcie Abraham, first published in *Reading the Bible as Asian Women* (CCA, 1986). Reprinted with permission.

'In the Beginning God Made the Word', by Ting Jin, first published in *Women in the New Creation* (AWRC, 1991). Reprinted with permission

The Pilgrim Press, Cleveland, Ohio 44115

Originally published by Sheffield Academic Press, Ltd., Sheffield, England

05 04 03 02 01 00   5 4 3 2 1

ISBN 0-8298-1399-3

Table of Contents

Editors' Preface

It is with great pleasure that we present the fourth in the Introductions in Feminist Theology Series. This series came to life as part of the work of the Britain and Ireland School of Feminist Theology which strives to create platforms for the dissemination of feminist theologies and thealogies. We are grateful to Sheffield Academic Press for enabling us to publish the journal of *Feminist Theology* as well as this series. We believe that both serve a useful purpose in the feminist arena.

Professor Kwok introduces us to a world of struggle, imagination, creativity and hope. She lays before us the many layered and diverse face of Asian feminist theologies. What the West has defined as Asia includes more than half the world's population and contains seven major languages and innumerable dialects. The racial and cultural mix under this broad title is immense and the economic realities are extremely varied. Almost half of Asia operates under communism while places like Hong Kong are examples of rampant capitalism.

Asia is a truly pluralist collection of societies and is of course the birthplace of many of the world's religions. Asian feminist theologians, if they are Christian, are part of a 3 per cent population, and have therefore to attend to religious diversity in a way quite unknown in Europe and America. They operate in cultures that have traditionally been accepting of new religions and respectful to older ones. They also carry out their theology in an epistemological world quite unlike our own. There is much decoding that needs to be done before dialogue can be entered into in a meaningful way between East and West. The conceptual worlds are poles apart. The strength of women's theology in Asia is that it is willing to embark on that task rather than attempt to find a common language and settle for the reduction in meaning that this often requires.

Professor Kwok is a skilled guide through these varied and exciting arenas. She engages us in the process of seeing the world differently and encourages us to delight in it. She smoothes our path but does not remove the hard questions.

This book lays before us the state of play in Asian theologies and tempts us to look to the future in tandem with the hopes, fears, struggles and triumphs of the peoples of Asia. We are delighted to have this book in our series.

Introduction

This book introduces the history, critical issues and direction of feminist theology in Asia. As a grassroots movement, Asian feminist theology began when Asian women gathered to discuss the Bible and their faith in the contexts of their own lives and Asian realities. Ever since the late 1970s, Asian Christian women have organized theological networks, convened ecumenical conferences, and begun to publish books and journals, contributing to feminist theologies emerging from the Third World. Participants in this movement include social activists, church reformers, community organizers, women priests and religious women, academics, theological students, and lay leaders of local churches. Beginning in the 1980s, associations of theologically trained women have been formed in various Asian countries, including Korea, Taiwan, Indonesia, India and the Philippines, and ecumenical networks have provided resources and support for the cross-fertilization of ideas and critical dialogues. Although the feminist theologians in Asia are few in number, they have made significant contributions to their churches and to the global feminist theological movement.

Not all women theologians in Asia want to be identified as feminist theologians. The term 'feminism' is controversial in some parts of Asia because it sometimes connotes a radicalism and separatism advocated by middle-class European and American women. Women in other parts of the world have identified their theology by other names. For example, African-American women have called their theology 'womanist theology', and some Hispanic women in the United States have begun calling the liberation theology of Hispanic women *mujerista* theology. Women theologians in Asia have not conjured up another name for the kind of liberation theology they are doing because there is no common language or concept they can use together. Many prefer to call their work Asian women's theology instead of feminist theology, to avoid the negative connotations of a militant, separatist and man-hating stance. But the term *feminism* is translated in my own Chinese language as 'women's rights movement', carrying a political overtone not found in other terms. I understand Asian feminist theology not only as a form of theological reflection but also as a political movement to transform the church and society so that women's freedom and dignity will be fully recognized.

Asian women comprise more than a quarter of the world's population. They live on a fascinating multilingual, multireligious and multiracial continent with diverse eating habits, ways of life and social and cultural realities. Asian feminist theology, shaped by such immense cultural and religious diversity, is pluralistic and multivocal, woven out of many separate strands. There is no one way of doing Asian feminist theology, and Asian feminist theologians in recent years have increasingly paid attention to their differences and not just their commonalities. To lift up the many voices of Asian feminist theologians, ample examples from different countries have been used throughout the book. Whenever possible, a brief statement is given about the background of the author in order to help readers understand the contexts from which the religious ideas come. Honoring the East Asian tradition, family names of Chinese and Korean authors are given in front of given names.

Chapter 1 surveys the diverse socio-political, religio-cultural and postcolonial contexts of Asia and articulates the challenges that Asian women face. The second chapter traces the emergence of feminist consciousness, analyzing the impact of Christianity on women's movements, the organization of women's theological networks, and the relationship between gospel and culture. Chapter 3 discusses the sources and resources of Asian feminist theology, with special attention to the use of women's experiences in theology, the interpretation of the Bible, and the appropriation of Asian religious traditions. Asian feminist interpretation of the Bible is the subject matter of Chapter 4, which presents numerous examples of Asian feminist hermeneutics as practiced in different countries: reclaiming women's heritage in the Bible, the oral interpretation and retelling of biblical stories, socio-political readings, postcolonial interpretations and scripture as performance.

Chapter 5 focuses on reconstructions of the concept of God within the religiously pluralistic context of Asia. It raises the issues of sexism versus more inclusive language, feminine images of the divine, and the understanding of God as the creative power of life. New images and metaphors for Christ offered by Asian feminist theologians from the Philippines, Korea, Hong Kong and India are presented in Chapter 6.

The issues of Christian imperialism, anthropocentric understandings of Christ, and reformulations of the doctrines of sin and redemption are discussed. The seventh chapter summarizes Asian women's critique of the patriarchal church and articulates their vision of the discipleship of women as well as equal partnership between women and men in church and society. The final chapter outlines the search for a passionate, life-affirming and empowering spirituality and its relationship to women's embodied selves and sexuality.

I would like to thank the Asian feminist theologians who have shared their ideas with me and supported my work for more than two decades. Grateful acknowledgment is due to Dr Lisa Isherwood, who invited me to contribute to the series and offered critical comments on the manuscript. Dr Beverly Moon, a scholar in comparative religions, edited the manuscript with great care and helped me to express my ideas with clarity. My research assistant, Anna Greenwood, offered much-needed help at the final stage of preparing the manuscript for publication. I am grateful to my colleagues at the Episcopal Divinity School for their friendship and to the school for providing generous support from the Theological Writing Fund.

Chapter One

Changing Asia: Promises and Crises

> Asia is a continent so diverse, so complex, so exhilarating that it is possible to only make broad generalizations about its socio-political, religio-cultural, economic contexts.
>
> Aruna Gnanadason (India)

More than half of the world's population live in Asia, a multicultural and multireligious continent that has undergone tremendous transformation during the past several decades. From Japan to Indonesia, and from the Philippines to Central Asia, people live in different socio-political realities and divergent cultural worlds. Divided into at least seven linguistic zones, Asia is also the birthplace of the major historical religions of humankind. For centuries, Asian people lived under the heavy yoke of the Portuguese, Spanish, British, French, Dutch, American and Japanese colonial powers. After World War II, many Asian peoples regained their independence, but their search for their national and cultural identities continues into the present.

In the past two decades, some of the Asian countries, especially those on the Pacific rim, have undergone rapid social and economic transformation. The increased linkage of these Asian economies to the global market has brought changes in cultural values, consumption patterns, life-styles and social expectations. But in other parts of Asia, hunger, famine and abject poverty are still overriding concerns. In India, for example, around 200 million people live in absolute poverty; in China, millions dwelling in the hinterland live at subsistence level, left out of the economic restructuring process taking place in the coastal cities. In many Asian countries, the opening of the market and increased foreign investment of multinational corporations create both opportunities and tremendous risks.

Economic and political changes in the Asian countries affect familial patterns, the status of women, reproduction and traditional gender roles. On the one hand, Asian women's access to education and growing participation in the labor market often lower the fertility rate, leading to the transformation of extended to nuclear families and increased participation of women in the decision-making process of the family. On the other hand, however, traditional cultural values of female subordination and domesticity still influence the social ethos, creating barriers to women's social advancement.

It is difficult to discuss the social and cultural contexts of Asian women's lives, because Asia is in perpetual flux. In many Asian cosmopolitan cities, we can see the juxtaposition of cultural elements from the East and the West, the ancient and the modern, the traditional and the avant-garde. When we analyze the situations of women in Asian societies, we need to take into consideration many factors, such as the rate of economic growth, the participation of women in the labor market, the changes in educational and family patterns and women's social and political involvements. Since the Asian societies are so diverse, we must guard against a generalized, monolithic and ahistorical image of the 'Asian woman'.

The Waterbuffalo and the Skyscraper: Multiple Asias

More than 70 per cent of the Chinese people are farmers; many still use waterbuffalo to till the land. In the Asian subcontinent, many struggle to survive because of poverty, malnutrition, the absence of safe drinking water, natural disasters and political and ethnic strife. Three-quarters of the world's illiterate population live in Asia. In Pakistan and Nepal, for example, 80 per cent of the women are illiterate, and in some parts of India and Bangladesh, about three-quarters of the women can barely read. Poverty, family responsibilities and other hardships drive many young Asian girls and women to sell their bodies for sexual services in the entertainment industries, in bars, nightclubs and discos, for example.

At the same time, in many Asian cities, such as Tokyo, Seoul, Hong Kong and Singapore, modern skyscrapers create magnificent skylines, as visible signs of economic boom and prosperity. These robust East Asian economies have led many observers to predict that the twenty-first century will be the 'Pacific Century'. According to a recent World Bank study, from 1965 to 1990 Asian economies grew faster than those of any other part of the world, well ahead of the industrial economies, about three times faster than Latin American and South Asian economies, and five times as fast as the economy of sub-Sahara Africa. Between 1965 and 1985, real income per capita more than quadrupled in Japan and in the so-called Four Little Dragons (South Korea, Taiwan, Hong Kong and Singapore) (*Far Eastern Economic Review* 1993: 51). In addition, other Southeast Asian countries, such as Thailand, Malaysia and Indonesia, have experienced phenomenal growth in the past decade, and China has emerged as the fastest growing economy in the world.

Yet uneven economic development in Asia raises questions about tradition and modernity, especially the modernization process as it assumes different cultural forms. Using Max Weber's theory, as developed in his *The Protestant Ethic and the Spirit of Capitalism*, scholars in Asia and the West have proposed that the Confucian tradition has exerted a decisive influence on the economic 'take off' of East Asia. Some emphasize the impact of Confucian ethics on the motivational structures, value systems, management theories and leadership patterns of both business and society. Since many Confucian values differ radically from the spirit of capitalism as identified by Weber, several Asian scholars enthusiastically suggest the possibility of a non-Western model of modernization bearing distinctively Confucian characteristics (see the discussion in Kwok 1995a: 133-45).

While Asian businessmen take pride in the Asian economic miracle for which scholars try to provide cultural and religious explanations, the plight of Asian women workers has largely been ignored. One of the major reasons for the competitiveness of Asian products in the global market is the availability of cheap labor, much of which comes from the increased participation of Asian women in the work force. Women are employed mostly in dead-end, low-skilled or semi-skilled manufacturing jobs, in retail and in the service sector. Close scrutiny of the wage structure in East Asian countries reveals that women generally earn less than men do: in Taiwan, women earn about 65 per cent of what men earn; in Hong Kong, about 74 per cent.

With the globalization of the market economy, multinational corporations find it profitable to relocate their factories in Third World countries. Thus, in the process of the international division of labor, women in Asia find low-paid, labor-intensive manufacturing jobs, especially in the textile and garment industries, the electronic industry and the toy industry. For example, the computer 'revolution', based on the development of semi-conductors and microprocessors, was made possible by relocating primarily American and Japanese firms to Southeast Asia, where women constitute up to 80 per cent of the work force in the electronic industries (Mies 1986: 113-14). Cheap female labor in developing countries is exploited in order to guarantee a constant supply of affordable goods for mass consumption in the rich and industrialized nations.

The economic development of Asian countries has been increasingly controlled by international financial institutions, such as the World Bank and the International Monetary Fund. The Asian economic crisis during 1997–98 has shown the vulnerability of these economies. Structural Adjustment packages were offered and Foreign Trade Zones were established to ensure that small nations become the nuts and bolts in a gigantic international economic machine. To protect the interests of foreign capital and the local national bourgeoisie, and in the name of national security, some countries have enacted laws limiting the organizing power of workers. Many women are employed in unsuitable and hazardous working conditions, where there is little protection under labor laws and where the management is dominated by men. Considered secondary or subsidiary labor, women are needed during an economic boom, but are easily laid off during economic recessions. In many Asian societies, there is little job security for female workers when they get sick, pregnant or become old. The varied pace of economic growth in Asian countries further creates a new class of migrant female workers. For example, a growing number of Filipino and Thai women are employed as domestics in the middle-class homes of Hong Kong and Singapore, taking care of household chores and children for working women there.

Women's work is also integrated into the agricultural sector of the world market. Instead of growing food for the family, many women are engaged in producing large-scale cash crops, such as rice, fruit, flowers and vegetables for export. Some work on tea or sugar plantations. Poor Sri Lankan girls and women pluck leaves for the British Lipton Tea Company, without ever dreaming of going to school, not to mention enjoying a cup of their finest Ceylon tea. Other women work as 'unpaid labor' in small peasant-run units and in farming cooperatives that produce for export. The mass production of cash crops requires constant use of chemical fertilizers, which destroy ecological balance and threaten a subsistence economy in which women play a major role.

The increased control of natural and human resources by international capital, the unchecked greed of Asian economic and political elites, and the misguided development policies of the past several decades have led to the breakdown of ecological balance in many Asian countries. In her *Staying Alive*, Indian physicist and ecologist Vandana Shiva links the violation of nature with the violation and marginalization of women, especially in Third World countries. She shows women's indispensable roles in the food chain and their significant contributions to the maintenance of a self-sufficient subsistence economy. The intervention of science and technology in the name of the green revolution and large-scale development projects, she argues, has led to hunger, malnutrition, the loss of economic control and a diminished quality of life for many women and their families. Shiva challenges women and men in Asia and in other parts of the world to work toward creating an ecological balance marked by harmony, sustainability and diversity (Shiva 1989).

The Local and the Global: The Search for Postcolonial Identity

In 1498 Vasco de Gama successfully found a route to the East and landed at Calicut, Kerala, on the West coast of India. Since the establishment of a Portuguese empire in India, with Goa as its capital, Asia has been drawn into a colonial orbit with Europe as its center. Successive waves of Western colonial powers arrived on Asian soil and subdued its people through military might, technological advance and economic strength. In 1800 the British empire consisted of 1.5 million square miles and 20 million people. By 1900 the Victorian empire was made up of 11 million square miles and about 390 million people. In the 1920s the West controlled almost half of the world's territory and total world population, many of whom lived in Asia (Huntington 1996: 51, 91). Along with the Western countries, Japan colonized Korea and Taiwan at the turn of the nineteenth century, following a period of modernization modeled after the West during the Meiji era.

Colonization brought into being an unequal power structure, reinforced by the ideologies of racial and cultural superiority. The colonial regimes introduced their own educational and social systems, their languages, and their religions as part of their 'civilizing mission' to the 'heathens'. The 'great century' of Christian mission coincided with the expansion of Western imperialism in the nineteenth century. Missionaries were sent to win souls for Christ, while bodies were colonized and foreign land violently confiscated. The Western invaders employed sexual images to romanticize the relationship of subordination and domination. The colonizers were often portrayed as the active and masculine, while the colonized were seen as passive and feminine. As one group of Asian women has noted:

> Western colonial culture taught us to accept the colonizers' superiority as a race and as a culture while denigrating our own as inferior, backward, and primitive. Moreover, the colonizers' characterization of Asian women as servile, weak, docile, long-suffering, delicate, and charming, and the idealization of these 'feminine' traits to best serve colonial goals, cemented the domination of men over women (EATWOT 1994: 19).

In the long and tortuous struggle for political independence and self-autonomy, Asian women have fought side by side with men and they have laid down their lives for freedom, human dignity and national integrity. For example, Filipino women joined their male counterparts in the struggle to overthrow the Spanish in the independence movement of 1898. Korean women and men fought long and hard for political autonomy after their country was colonized by Japan in 1895. In China, the early twentieth century saw the end of a millennia-old monarchy and the struggle for independence from foreign encroachment. Female students took to the streets with their male classmates during the famous May Fourth Movement of 1919.

However, women's roles in the struggle for independence have been downplayed by both male elites and historians, for whom regaining political autonomy meant not so much the liberation of the people as a whole, but rather the overthrow of foreign masters and the redeeming of 'Asian manhood'. During the struggle for independence, Asian women were repeatedly told to put women's issues on the back burner for the sake of the common good, while after independence, Asian politics were dictated primarily by men: local patriarchs, the military and big businesses. In the name of national security, martial law was declared for long periods of time in Korea, in the Philippines and in Taiwan. The rightful aspirations of the powerless and the voiceless, including many women, for democracy, justice and freedom were brutally suppressed.

During national rebuilding in the wake of independence, Asian women were exhorted to contribute to national development and modernization while at the same time confined by traditional Asian female virtues of self-sacrifice, obedience and subservience. The struggle for women's autonomy has been criticized repeatedly as both Western and bourgeois, not applicable nor desirable in the Asian context. The myth of Asian national cultures, as something inherently different from that found in the West has served to keep Asian women in line. We have seen how Confucian ideology has been uncritically revived to explain the East Asian economic wonder, which is based on the exploitation of women. Likewise, in other parts of Asia, fundamentalist movements within Islam and Hinduism have emerged in recent years, subscribing often to stereotypical views of male dominance.

But as postcolonial critics have pointed out, it is not really possible to recover an uncorrupted or undefiled Asian national or cultural identity that predates the arrival of Western influences. One of the traumatic characteristics of the 'colonial experience' is that one does not feel at home even in one's own homeland. Often one experiences feelings of displacement and fragmentation, along with a deep sense of alienation. Instead of trying to subscribe to an imaginary homogenous and coherent national culture, it may be more fruitful to examine how cultural identity is constructed over time, and to pay attention to the interplay between history, culture and power. The past should not be resurrected in order to justify oppression in the present, but rather it should be retold to enable the liberation of all. As Stuart Hall, a black Jamaican theorist who has written extensively on race, colonialism and culture, has said:

> Far from being grounded in a mere 'recovery' of the past, which is wait-
> ing to be found, and which, when found, will secure our sense of our-
> selves into eternity, identities are the names we give to the different ways
> we are positioned by, and position ourselves within, the narratives of the
> past (Hall 1990: 225).

Asian women, many of whom have seldom been allowed to participate in retelling or refashioning the past, must claim the right to do so. On the one hand, Asian women have to question the 'master narratives', which present the history of the colonized as a mere extension of the history of the colonizers. On the other hand, they have to challenge another form of 'master narrative', created by their male counterparts to justify the norm of male supremacy. Moreover, Asian women must be sensitive to the diversity among women created by class, ethnicity, religion, local histories and cultures. They have to be politically astute to discern that gender oppression has been imbued with different meanings during different historical epochs. For example, the oppression of Asian women was emphasized by colonial masters to justify their mission of 'saving yellow women from the yellow men'. Meanwhile, in the post-colonial period, the subordination of Asian women has served as a signifier of 'authentic' Asian cultural characteristic. Critiquing both the normative history of the West and the androcentric nationalistic Asian narratives, Asian women in divergent contexts have to plot pluralistic counter-histories and project new visions of their identities.

As has been pointed out, the old form of colonialism has given way to neocolonialism, which seeks to dominate the world through the creation of a single, global financial or capital market. Globalization not only takes the form of economic control, as in the financing of huge Third World debts, but also in global control of mass media, the promotion of Western life-styles and militarization. Since the disintegration of the former Soviet Union and the transformation of Eastern Europe, the United States has emerged as the sole superpower. American products, such as MacDonald's hamburgers, Coca-Cola and blue jeans, dominate the world market, while CNN and other American news media interpret world events according to American perspectives. Fueled by the information superhighway, globalization seeks to create a universal capitalist monoculture unaffected by national boundaries. This transnational process is not accountable to the masses, who may struggle to have some democratic participation in national politics, but have little influence in the decision-making processes of transnational corporations.

The latest form of neocolonialism rules, not so much through force and coercion, but rather by the power of seduction, persuasion and the production of desire. The dominant images of women in the global mass media include woman as sexual object and consumer. All over the world women are told to model themselves after the life-styles of Western women and to desire what Western women are supposed to desire. Thus, Asian women defining their own identity and destiny have to fight a two-pronged battle. On the one hand, they have to challenge stereotypical images of Asian women of the past as constructed by Asian male elites; and on the other, they have to guard the future from images of womanhood as prescribed by the global mass media. In a postcolonial context, the Asian woman is not quite 'authentically' Asian, while at the same time she is not quite 'Western' enough. She is always falling in-between. Nevertheless, it is this 'in-between' space that opens up new possibilities for negotiating identity, exploring cultural hybridity and articulating different cultural practices and priorities.

The Virtuous Woman and the Whore: Sexual Violence against Women

The pain and suffering of colonization and military aggression is often inscribed on the bodies of women through sexual violence, rape and torture. During World War II, for example, both Korea and Taiwan suffered under the harsh and oppressive colonial rule of Japan. To satisfy the sexual appetite of the Japanese soldiers located throughout the Asian and Pacific region, somewhere between 100,000 and 200,000 Korean women were forcibly drafted to serve as 'comfort women'. Some of these Korean women were kidnapped from their homes, while others were promised jobs working in military restaurants or as domestic maids. In addition to Korean women, women from China, Taiwan, Hong Kong, the Philippines, Vietnam, Indonesia and Japan were likewise enlisted and exploited. According to the recent testimonies of former comfort women, they were made to serve an average of 30–40 soldiers per day, with little in the way of food or compensation. Comfort women suffered unspeakable crimes and extreme suffering, including beatings and torture, widespread venereal disease, abortions, death and massive abandonment after the defeat of Japan. After the war, the Japanese government repeatedly denied that such large-scale sexual exploitation had occurred, while leaders of Asian countries refused to pursue the issue because of the feelings of national humiliation and the need to court Japanese capital. Only on account of sustained pressure from women's organizations in Korea and in other Asian countries did Japan finally admit to these crimes and did the comfort women's issue receive international attention.

Sexual exploitation of Asian women took a different form and became institutionalized during the Vietnam War when Southeast Asia became the 'rest and recreation' center for American soldiers. Young women and girls provided sexual services in bars, massage parlors, nightclubs and brothels situated near military bases. After the war sex tourism flourished in many Asian countries and brought in much needed foreign capital. For example, so-called 'tourism' has become the largest industry in Thailand, superseding the export of rice. From 1965 to 1988, the number of tourists increased from 250,000 to 4,250,000. Defining prostitution as a form of sexual labor, Vietnamese scholar Thanh-dam Truong documents the vast international network that keeps the sex industry going, including local police, gangs and pimps, government officials, the international tourist market, the airline industry, advertising, hotel and food services, and even the World Bank, through financing development projects (Truong 1990).

Today, the sex industry in Asia is highly developed and assumes many different forms: the traditional type of street walkers and brothels, the international trafficking of women, sex tourism, prostitution around military bases, child prostitution, and affluent society prostitution. According to a recent study by Rita Nakashima Brock and Susan Brooks Thistlethwaite, prostitution is sustained by numerous factors: economic exploitation, the social structure of male dominance, the legal protection of patrimony, the cultivation of hypermasculine cultures and androcentric religious teachings (1996). Since the spread of the AIDS epidemic in the 1980s, many prostitutes in Southeast Asian countries have contracted the virus but received little medical care. Fearing contagion, more and more customers in the flesh trade prefer younger children, both girls and boys. Child prostitution is on the rise, with children as young as two or three used in parts of Asia.

While numerous Asian women are selling their bodies to increase the Gross National Product, Asian women in general are exhorted to be chaste, faithful and respectable as defined by cultural and religious norms. The polarization of virtuous woman or whore serves to divide women into different classes. Considered a source of temptation for men, women's sexuality is looked on as a power that must be guided and brought under control. Before marriage, a woman is considered the property of the father; after marriage, the husband has ownership of her body and her children. The patriarchal family institution, the churches and other religious organizations, the cultural ethos and government policies join hand in hand to keep women submissive and in their place. For example, arranged marriage is still widely practiced in parts of India, and the dowry system, which requires the bride's family to pay cash or goods to the groom's family, has inflicted suffering on many girls and women. In China, where the socialist regime fails to integrate adequately matters of gender into its Marxist analysis, the Women's Federation is very much under the influence of the government. Because of the magnitude of China's population problem, the government has sought to police women's reproduction through stringent birth-control regulations and the one-child policy. In the Philippines, where the majority of the population is Roman Catholic, the church promulgates conservative views on family planning and divorce. In Muslim countries, such as Malaysia, Indonesia and Pakistan, the revival of fundamentalistic movements compels women to cover their heads and observe strict sexual codes.

Women's struggle for freedom has been systematically silenced through domestic violence, rape, public censure, imprisonment and torture. For example, Taslima Nasreen from Bangladesh was issued a death threat and had to flee her country for daring to challenge the teachings of women's subordination in the Qu'ran. Democracy advocate Aung San Suu Kyi of Burma has been placed under house arrest and separated from her husband and family for years. When a group of Asian women theologians met in 1994 to discuss women's struggle against violence, they recounted stories of escalating sexual violence, rape and wife-beating in some parts of Asia. In 1993 in Madras, a woman, whose family could pay only part of her dowry, was ordered to have an abortion. When she refused, she was killed by having acid forced down her throat. In Olongapo City in the Philippines, a 13-year-old prostitute died of an infection in her uterus caused by a broken vibrator that was left inside her body by a tourist. In Marsinah, Indonesia, a female leader of workers was found dead in the forest, having been brutally battered, with a pipe through her vagina (EATWOT 1994: 15).

The multiple oppression of women in Asia has called for a response by women's organizations, civic groups and churches. Since the late 1970s, progressive women's groups have been formed in many Asian countries and new feminist movements are emerging. These groups work for economic and political liberation from oppression, as well as liberation from sexual discrimination based on patriarchy (Matsui 1989: 143-57). In the Philippines, a national organization of more than 70 groups of women, GABRIELA, was formed in 1984 to work for more stringent laws prohibiting the sex industry, to press for the punishment of users and traffickers of women and children and to provide alternative jobs for prostitutes. GABRIELA played a crucial role during the 'people power' revolution in 1986, toppling the long-lasting Marcos dictatorship. In Thailand, women's groups established the New Life Centers for prostitutes, and organizations such as Foundation for Women, Empower, and the Association for the Promotion of the Status of Women, have demanded changes in the law and have worked for the social and economic empowerment of women. Progressive Japanese women's groups, such as Asian Women's Association founded in 1977, have also worked in solidarity with Korean and Southeast Asian women to stop sex tourism and the trafficking of women.

In Korea, women's groups have combated dictatorship and labored for better employment conditions for women workers. In 1983 a Women's Hotline was established to provide support and counseling for battered women and to launch campaigns against domestic violence. In 1991, Korean feminists formed the Korean Council for Women Drafted for Sexual Slavery by Japan and pushed the 'comfort women' issue into the national and international limelight. In Taiwan, progressive women's groups have promoted democracy, self-autonomy and political participation in the government. The Rainbow project was established in the 1980s to fight the selling and coercion of young tribal girls for prostitution in urban cities. Recently, women's groups have participated in the environmental movement, the consumers movement and educational reforms. In Hong Kong, the Society for the Advancement of Women's Status was formed in 1984 to promote feminist consciousness and to effect policy changes. Additional grassroots women's groups were formed to organize women workers. During the transitional period, when Hong Kong returned to China in 1997, a coalition of women's groups worked closely with other political organizations to ensure freedom and democracy in Hong Kong's future.

As Asian women gradually move out from the confines of the home to exert more power in the public sphere, they have become a new force shaping Asian politics and society. In Pakistan, India, Bangladesh and Burma, women have been top government officials or leaders of political parties. In other parts of Asia, women have been active in democratic movements to bring about fundamental social and political changes. Transforming silence into action, some Christian women have expressed their vision of a wholistic liberation embracing humanity and mother earth:

> Women's empowerment entails the development of an alternative paradigm over and against the life-effacing processes of patriarchy, capitalism, and First World-oriented maldevelopment. Women's paradigm of new society is based on wholeness of life. It is cosmic-centered and sustains all forms of life. It is a spiritual quest to regain our identity, that we are born of the earth and are partners with creation. Women's movements have thus emerged to respond to global as well as local needs. These movements manifest a new way of exercising power through collective dialogue and participatory action (EATWOT 1994: 25).

As we face the twenty-first century, Asian women will play an increasing role in shaping the future development of Asia and the direction this most populous continent will take.

Chapter Two

The Emergence of Feminist Theological Consciousness

Her personal encounter with God is denounced as heretical or hysterical: if the first, she is figuratively burnt at the stake; if the second, people hasten to find her a husband.

Marianne Katoppo (Indonesia)

In 1979 Marianne Katoppo, an award-winning novelist and theologian from Indonesia, published the first book of Asian feminist theology in English. Entitled *Compassionate and Free*, the volume criticized patriarchal religion and society and called for a life-giving theology that affirms women's dignity (Katoppo 1979). In 1991 the global Christian Church was stunned when a young feminist theologian from Korea gave a moving and powerful keynote address at the seventh assembly of the World Council of Churches. After invoking the spirits of the people who had died in Hiroshima and Nagasaki, in the gas chambers of the Holocaust, in Kwang-ju, Tiananmen Square, and Lithuania, Chung Hyun Kyung began her address with a shamanistic ritual that involved burning a scroll (Chung 1991: 37-47).

Chung's presentation demonstrated the need for a paradigmatic shift in doing theology, as she analyzed the multiple oppression of women living under sexism, classism and neocolonialism from an Asian perspective. She freely employed both indigenous rituals and Asian philosophical themes and cultural motifs to articulate the hope and aspirations of Asian people. Her daring and breath-taking voice challenged many of the established norms of doing theology and gave an unequivocal signal that a new women's theology was emerging in Asia.

The Birth of a New Theological Consciousness

Chung's provocative presentation must be understood in the wider context of the development of feminist theological consciousness in Asia.

Although in early periods Asian Christian women had reflected on their faith, a collective, conscious attempt to do Asian feminist liberation theology did not begin until the late 1970s. Since then, Asian women have formed theological networks and organized their own theological consultations to share resource materials, to stimulate creative theological thinking and to publish their own theological writings.

For some of the Asian women theologians, the emergence of a feminist awareness is closely related to their personal history and the suffering in their own lives. Born into a wealthy family, Chung Hyun Kyung was ostracized by her affluent classmates in high school when her father suddenly went bankrupt and lost all the family's possessions. Chung's feminist consciousness was heightened when she finally met with her birth mother, who had been hidden from her for more than 30 years (Chung 1990: 1-5). For Marianne Katoppo, her experience of being the Other as a Christian woman in a predominantly Muslim society prompted her to write *Compassionate and Free*, where she describes her experience as follows:

> I found that to be the Other was an alienating experience: the Christian among the Muslims, the westernized Minahassan who was out of place in a Javanese society, the girl who was taught to look upon boys as equals, not as superiors (1979: 5).

As the Other in their own society, these Asian women became more conscious of the suffering of those who are marginalized when they engaged in the struggle for liberation of their people. Chung Hyun Kyung learned the nature of neocolonialism and the systemic exploitation of the poor when she participated in the student movement against the dictatorial government during her college years. Mary John Mananzan, a Benedictine sister from the Philippines, was drawn away from her comfortable position as a teacher of contemporary philosophy in a Jesuit university to join the first workers' strike in 1975, after the declaration of martial law. Together with workers and slum dwellers, she had her first encounter with military brutality and she experienced helplessness before the reality of sheer force and institutionalized violence (Mananzan 1989: 102).

As these women began to analyze their social and political situations, they became aware that women in impoverished countries are the poor among the poor, the voiceless among the voiceless. Mananzan was concerned with prostitution in the Philippines for some time when she co-founded in 1978 the *Filipina*, the first feminist organization in the Philippines, and established the Center for Women Resources. Subsequently she became the chairperson of GABRIELA and continued to be deeply involved in feminist theology in Asia and in the Third World. Aruna Gnanadason, the former executive secretary of the All India Council of Christian Women, now works for the World Council of Churches. Because of her earlier Marxist orientation, she has put the liberation of the working class as a priority. She was critical of the feminists for dividing the working class. But when she was criticized by the women for failing to take into consideration the suffering of the second sex, she found her voice as a woman for the first time. She recalled many years later: 'It was a real transformation I went through... I discovered this system of patriarchy and my whole analysis changed. I realized how inadequate my Marxist analysis had been' (Fabella 1993: 82).

Other women experienced similar transformations when they discovered sexism in the movements for democracy. Sun Ai Lee Park, a minister and theologian from Korea, observed: 'There were these Korean men working for democracy and human rights in Korea. They said they want democracy in the country, but when it came to women, it was something else! I started wondering what kind of democracy they were looking for' (Fabella 1993: 88). In the early 1970s, I began my involvement in the student movement in Hong Kong, fighting for Chinese as an official language, in addition to English. During that period, I became aware of different social theories and began to do comparative analysis of women's status in socialist China and capitalist Hong Kong. Gradually a growing number of Asian Christian women in different countries realized that women's liberation could not be subordinated to the overall liberation of the people, as Mananzan emphatically stated:

> There is no total human liberation without the liberation of women in society. And this is not an automatic consequence of either economic development or political revolution. In other words, the women's movement is an essential aspect of the very process of societal liberation (Mananzan 1989: 105).

This critical awareness caused them to raise fundamental questions concerning the kind of theological education they had received and the adequacy of any theological system that does not take women's issues seriously. Trained in linguistic philosophy in Rome and in Münster, Mananzan later recalled that her theological training had been very Germanic, failing to touch on women's problems. Her experience was echoed by Chung, who says:

> Throughout my eleven years of theological training, I have written
> countless term papers and theological essays for highly educated people
> who were my teachers... I no longer want to write so-called 'compre-
> hensive' theology seeking to answer questions of privileged Europeans. I
> want to do theology in solidarity with and in love for my mother so as to
> resurrect crucified persons—like her—by giving voice to their hurts and
> pains (Chung 1990: 5).

With the creation of theological networks, the individual quest of
Asian women for an Asian feminist liberation theology became a shared
vision and a collective endeavor. The Conference of Theologically
Trained Women of Asia was organized in January 1981 by the Christian
Conference of Asia. The Women's Desk was formed with Elizabeth
Tapia, a Methodist minister from the Philippines, as the first staff person.
The Women's Commission of the Ecumenical Association of Third
World Theologians (EATWOT) was formed in 1983, and Asian female
members had a forum to discuss their issues and to dialogue with
women from other Third World countries. Sun Ai Lee Park had the
vision to launch the Asian women's theological journal *In God's Image*
in 1982 and was instrumental in the formation of Asian Women's
Resource Centre for Culture and Theology in 1988. During 1980s
associations of theologically trained Women were established in various
countries of Asia, such as Korea, Taiwan, Indonesia and India. Since
then Asian women theologians have met regionally and nationally to
analyze patriarchy in the church and in society, to discuss strategies for
women's struggle, and to discover resources for doing theology. In 1985
Asian women gathered in Manila to discuss the theme 'Total Liberation
from the Perspective of Asian Women'. Two years later, a conference
on 'Doing Theology as Asian Women' was held in Singapore. In the
summer of 1990 in Seoul and around Christmas in 1991 in Madras,
members of EATWOT met to search for Asian feminist hermeneutical
principles in interpreting the Bible.

Asian women theologians have been aware of the need to learn from
other Asian religious traditions. In 1988, the rich tradition of feminine
images of the divine in Asia was discussed in a small meeting in Hong
Kong. In 1989, the first Asian Women's Consultation on Interfaith Dialogue took place in Kuala Lumpur in Malaysia, a city well known for its
multicultural and multireligious setting. The Consultation succeeded in
bringing together Muslim, Buddhist, Hindu and Christian women in
Asia to reflect on how Asian religions have shaped the cultures of Asian
countries. The Christian women present were especially interested to

learn about gender construction in other religions and the liberative elements for women (Abraham *et al.* 1989b: 3). The Consultation was meant to be the beginning of an ongoing process of study. A second consultation took place in Sri Lanka in 1991. Through these interreligious dialogues, Asian women theologians gained insights into how to articulate feminist theology from a multireligious context.

The EATWOT network enables Asian feminist theologians to meet with and learn from other feminist theologians of the Third World. Virginia Fabella, a Maryknoll sister from the Philippines, has been with EATWOT since the beginning and has documented the struggle of women within the organization (Fabella 1993). The first intercontinental women's conference took place in Oaxtepec, Mexico, in 1986, and the papers were gathered as a best-selling collection, *With Passion and Compassion* (Fabella and Oduyoye 1988). A dialogue with First World women has been discussed in ecumenical circles for many years and the conference finally convened in Costa Rica in 1994 with the theme 'Spirituality for Life: Women Struggling against Violence' (Mananzan *et al.* 1996). Some Asian feminist theologians have also been active in ecumenical movements in Asia, with the World Council of Churches and denominational networks.

Claiming the Authority to Do Theology

Many churches in Asia were established as a result of missionary activities originating in Europe and North America during the nineteenth century. Although Asian countries have become independent, there is still the colonial legacy of looking toward the West for guidance and tutoring. This is especially evident in the liturgy, organization and life of Christian churches in Asia. For a long time, theologians read Barth, Brunner and Tillich, trying to solve theological puzzles for other contexts, with little or no relevance for Asia. This theological dependency has had devastating effects on the witness and mission of the Asian churches. After centuries of missionary effort, less than 3 per cent of the population in Asia claim to be Christian, while the majority still see Christianity as a foreign religion, even if not condemning it as the religion of the oppressors.

Political independence has ushered in a new awareness of Asian culture and history, and various attempts of indigenization of theology into Asian soil have taken place since the 1960s. Asian theologians including

M.M. Thomas of India, Kosuke Koyama of Japan and D.T. Niles of Sri Lanka have urged their colleagues to construct Waterbuffalo Theology, and to do theology in the midst of the Asian revolutions. Laudable for their nationalism and cultural pride, these attempts, nevertheless, have reinforced a rather homogeneous and patriarchal understanding of Asia's past. Challenging the colonial legacy, these theologians sometimes were too eager to embrace the cultural traditions of Asia, without taking sufficient notice of their elitist and sexist components. In the preoccupation with lifting up their own theological voices, they have failed to be concerned with the liberation of women, which would have required them to face their own sexist values.

Because of the hierarchical and patriarchal church structure, many denominations in Asia still do not ordain women. The number of female theological students, though on the rise, remains small, and few Asian women receive advanced degrees in theology. When the feminist consciousness of Asian Christian women was heightened, they began to look for new models for doing theology, since they were no longer able to accept the one-sided views of their male professors and colleagues. Some of them had been exposed to the feminist theologies developed by Europeans and European Americans beginning in the 1970s. But they quickly discovered that white, middle-class feminist theologies were not relevant for Asian women without first being radically challenged. First, the Western feminist theologies speak from within a cultural context in which Christianity is the dominant tradition, whereas everywhere in Asia, except in the Philippines and South Korea, Christians are but a tiny minority. Second, earlier feminist theologies had a tendency to universalize the Western women's experiences as if they represented the lives of all women. The failure to respect difference and the constant incorporation of the Other into one's own perspective are rooted in the social and cultural matrix of colonialism. Third, the feminist analyses as proposed by white, middle-class women are not radical enough. Narrowly defining patriarchy as the domination of men over women, these analyses fail to provide tools to examine colonialism, cultural imperialism, religious pluralism and the horizontal violence of women against women. Fourth, some of these feminist theologians display racist and ethnocentric orientations, even while calling for a global sisterhood. For example, in her global study of sado-rituals done against women, Mary Daly can only imagine Indian women as burned-alive, immolated objects, Chinese women as eroticized foot-bound objects, and African women as genitally mutilated objects. She argues: 'Those who claim to see racism and/or imperialism in my indictment of those atrocities can do so only by blinding themselves to the fact that the oppression of women knows no ethnic, national, or religious bounds' (Daly 1978: 111). While these atrocities did and continue to exist in some places, her study nowhere presents Third World women as agents to change their plight, and to work for a better future.

Christian feminists in Asia realize that they cannot be the gentle, passive and exotic females as portrayed in the global mass media; and neither can they be targets of Christian mission, nor eroticized objects in other people's theological imagination. They must claim back the authority to be *theological subjects*, reflecting on God's liberating activities in Asia and articulating their own theology. Instead of passively consuming a male-oriented and Eurocentric theological tradition, they must challenge the past as they envision a new future. In the words of one group of Asian feminist theologians:

> we recognized that the classical, Western, colonial, feudalistic, elite, and patriarchal theologies passed on to us have themselves inflicted much violence on women's life. These theologies have misogynistic texts of terror and tradition at the core. Furthermore, they have separated theology from spirituality, piety from social action for justice, and intellectual reflection from its symbolic expression in ritual and art (EATWOT 1994: 21).

These same women have criticized the patriarchal church for failing to live up to its prophetic witness, while at the same time reproaching male Asian theologians for refusing to deal with women's issues honestly. Clearly any theology from Asia that leaves out half the population is limited in scope; and its potential for radical change compromised. Unless the multiply oppressed Asian women are free, all are not free. Any liberation theology that claims to liberate the poor and the non-person is itself in need of liberation, if it fails to address the plight of prostitutes, battered women, female political prisoners and women who are forced to have abortions. In the introduction to an anthology of Asian women's theological writings, Virginia Fabella and Sun Ai Lee Park make the point clearly:

> Unless our thoughts as women are known and our voices heard, the work towards rearticulating Christian theology in Asia will remain truncated. God's face will only be half seen and God's voice only half heard. If the emerging Asian theology is to be significant to men and women alike, our contribution as Asian women cannot be isolated or simply

> attached as a token appendage, but must form an integral part of the
> whole (Fabella and Park 1989: ix-x).

For many Asian feminist theologians, theology is not simply an intellectual discipline or a rational reflection of Christian faith. Theologians cannot afford to engage in the academic exercise of mental gymnastics, when so many people are daily dehumanized or die of malnutrition and unsafe drinking water. Theology must be embodied; and reflection and action must be integrally linked together.

Furthermore, in Asia theology is not done within the confines of the Christian community. Its audience is not limited to members of the Church. Such a theological focus is too narrow and unwarranted on a continent where the percentage of Christians is so small. Asian feminist theologians work closely with other secular feminists and civic and revolutionary leaders, who constantly call them to account for their faith.

Theology emerging from the womb of Asia must simultaneously address people's suffering and articulate their hope and aspirations. As I have written in an earlier essay:

> feminist theology in Asia will be a cry, a plea and invocation. It emerges
> from the wounds that hurt, the scars that hardly disappear, the stories that
> have no ending. Feminist theology in Asia is not written with a pen, it is
> inscribed on the hearts of many that feel the pain, and yet dare to hope
> (Kwok 1984: 228).

Listening to the cries of women, Asian feminist theologians take into serious consideration their individual perspectives on reality. They have learned to look at history from the underside. For this reason, they have found that neither Aristotelian logic, Aquinas's dialectics, nor Tillich's method of correlation are adequate to help them to articulate the theological aspirations of Asian women. In order to artfully present their rich, multilayered and polyphonic theological voices, they have to engage in new myth-making, symbol-creating and story-telling. Yet such an imaginative usage of the cultural resources of Asian people has been labeled 'syncretistic', especially since Chung Hyun Kyung's controversial presentation in Canberra. Critics have completely forgotten that a long time ago Rudolf Bultmann called Christianity syncretistic, without any negative connotations (Bultmann 1956: 177-79). In fact, it was the adaptation of Christianity to its Hellenistic setting and its ability to assimilate new elements that made it a viable tradition. In the history of Christianity, numerous 'pagan' practices were adopted, including Santa Claus, the Easter rabbit and the Christmas tree. Most Christians do not condemn these practices as syncretistic, or raise concerns that Aquinas employed Aristotelian philosophy and Schleiermacher used Romantic thought. But when daring feminist theologians from Asia use new styles in their expression of faith, they are silenced and labeled syncretistic, or even heretical!

But for Chung, Mananzan, Gnanadason, and others like them, whose faith has been repeatedly tested in the baptism of fire, such name-calling and censorship will not deter them from challenging the status quo, and proclaiming a spirituality for life. Like the Hebrew prophets and the psalmists, they know that neither the challenge they face nor its difficulty are new. Indeed, no fewer than three psalms begin by urging 'O sing to the Lord a new song' (Pss. 96, 98, 149); likewise, Isaiah admonishes: 'Sing to the Lord a new song, his praise from the end of the earth' (Isa. 42.10) (Bell 1992: 145-46).

The Relation of Gospel and Culture

Among the theological issues that have emerged from discussions among Asian feminist theologians in recent years, the most critical is the relationship between the gospel and culture. The Jesus movement first emerged as a reform movement within Judaism. As Christianity spread throughout the Mediterranean world in the first century, it encountered the fascinating, multicultural and multireligious Hellenistic world. Early Christian writers used Greek philosophical concepts and Gnostic categories to express their new faith. The Christian community did not hesitate to retain both Jewish and other Near Eastern religious symbols, rituals and practices. In its two thousand years of history, Christianity continued to learn from and appropriate cultural forms from different parts of the world.

But the encounter of Christianity with *women's culture* has always been deemed suspect by the patriarchal church hierarchy. Women's voices were effectively left out when the male writers turned oral traditions into written biblical narratives. Scanty records of women in the early church were preserved, and most of them were women martyrs. It was as if women could only be allowed to 'speak' if they died. Later in Christendom, radical and unruly women were burned as witches, and the religious visions and writings of women mystics were considered to be less important than the theological treatises of men. Women's religious communities were treated as secondary and subordinate, and female founders of religious movements, such as Mary Eddy Baker, did

not receive their due respect. Given this past, it should not surprise any-
one that the contemporary male church hierarchy finds it alarming that
feminist theologians from the Third World are talking about God, and
using idioms and symbols from cultures historically not shaped by the
Christian tradition to do so.

Asian feminist theologians are emboldened by the fact that many
Christian women in different historical epochs have resisted the monolithic understanding of God as defined by malestream culture, reflecting
the experiences of men only. Claiming the power to do theology, they
have questioned earlier models of indigenization or contextualization
that sought to bridge gospel and culture in the Asian context. First,
these earlier attempts usually assumed that there was a privileged origin,
a pure essence, or a body of normative texts that could be lifted out of
its original context and transplanted into Asia. Second, the Asian soil
that was to receive such an uncorrupted or pure Christianity was either
a cultural context defined by male and elitist Asian traditions or a socio-
political context defined by male nationalistic liberation movements.

To conceptualize the multiplicity and fluidity of the relationship
between gospel and culture, I would like to use the concepts of cultural
translation, cultural hybridization and cultural resistance, as developed in
postcolonial theory. *Translation* here means rearticulation, transcoding or
transculturation. It does not imply one original text of which the 'translation' is but a mere copy. As Stuart Hall has said, translation is a 'continuous process of re-articulation and re-contextualization, without any
notion of a primary origin' (Hall 1996b: 393). The Gospel writers, Paul,
the Johannine circles and the Qumran community were involved in
this cultural translation process, as the Christian theologians have been
throughout the centuries. In his study of African Christianity, Lamin
Sanneh has shown that the translation of the Bible and the Christian
message into the vernacular during the missionary movement has further
promoted plurality and cultural particularity (Sanneh 1989: 233-34).
Unlike Islam, which maintains that Arabic is the sacred language, Christianity assumes that the Christian faith can be expressed in all the languages and cultures of humankind.

The claim to possess, to represent, to speak for, or to be closer than
others to the 'primary origin' is imbued with the desire for power. During the colonial period, cultural practices of the 'Mother Churches' in
the West were duplicated and re-enacted all over the world. Even
today, some of the Anglican churches in Africa still use the Common

Prayer Book of 1662. Before Vatican II, the catholicity of the Roman Catholic Church was guaranteed by the Latin Rite, as well as the uniformity of church structure. The Bible, regarded largely by Christians as the primary text, is still taken to be the norm or criterion to judge all other cultures and civilizations. The voices of women and their aspirations for ordination were silenced because the original 12 apostles were all male, and the patrilineal line of authority was secured by apostolic succession.

This concept of cultural translation allows Asian women to relativize the truth claims of ethnocentric missionaries, male theologians of all races, cultures, hues, and stripes, and white, middle-class feminists. No theological system can claim to be universally valid because it is closer to the 'origin'. From the outset theology has been a human construction conditioned by cultural specificity, linguistic option, historical circumstances and theological imagination. Western models of theology are but expressions of this transcultural and transcoding process, and should not be the norm for everybody. Furthermore, Edward Said has convincingly argued that the justification of empire-building undergirded Western cultural imagination in the nineteenth and early twentieth century, influencing the high cultures of scholarship, novels and the arts. The construction of Western theology during this critical period of colonial expansion must be questioned in so far as it, too, was shaped by the ethos of empire-building. Colonization is a double inscription process, affecting the colonizers as much as the colonized.

Second, the notion of cultural hybridization allows us to talk about the imaginative weaving and blending of cultural fragments, religious motifs and people's memories in the conceptualization of self, the world and God. The colonial experience has left a long-lasting imprint on former colonies, and the 'post-colonial' world has always been 'diasporic' in relation to what might be its cultures of origin (Hall 1996a: 250). In addition, Asians have lived for millennia in a multicultural context, and mixing and borrowing among different cultural and religious traditions has been the rule. Christianity assumed a new form and spoke a new language when brought into dialogue with Confucian classics, the Vedas and the *Dao de jing* in past attempts of indigenization by male theologians. Today, Asian feminist theologians lift up the multivocal nature of Asian traditions and begin new lines of theological inquiry by rearticulating theology through the liberating language of myths, stories and the rituals of women. As Chung Hyun Kyung has said:

Male leaders of the institutional church always seem preoccupied with
the doctrinal purity of their religions. What matters to Asian women is
survival and the liberation of themselves and their communities... Asian
women selectively have chosen life-giving elements of their culture and
religions and have woven new patterns of religious meaning (Chung
1990: 113).

Finally, cultural hybridization suggests that cultures are not isolated,
self-contained entities, distinctly separated from each other. Cultural
identity is formed in a complex process of claiming one's position within
a network of relationships and telling the narrative that gives one meaning, while listening to many other narratives. This means that Asian
feminist theologians cannot afford to do theology from within their specific contexts alone, without dialogues with traditional male theology,
feminist theology from different parts of the world and Asian male
theology. Yet, Asian feminist theology should not be a copy or a weak
mimicry of other people's theology. Just as translation involves expressing meaning in one's own categories and thought forms, Asian feminist
theologians must claim the power to speak their own theological dialects
in order to be theological subjects. Since there are literally thousands of
dialects in Asia, there is no single way of doing feminist theology. Feminist theology in the Asian context will be multilingual, pluralistic and
radically open to new challenges and possibilities.

The notion of cultural resistance is critical in our contemporary world,
where new information technology, consumerism, multinational corporations, the international division of labor and the weakening of national
boundaries seek to create a transnational capitalist culture, defined by
the interests of global capital. Furthermore, fundamentalist groups and
American tele-evangelists have used the latest technology to get their
messages across the world. Asian feminist theologians, together with
other marginalized groups, must continue to strive for social and cultural
space to articulate their own theology. They must be vigilant as this new
global capitalist culture is shaped not only by European and North
American elites, but also by the Asian bourgeoisie who are trying to get
their market share. The glorification of national culture (as in the case of
Confucian elites in East Asia) can be used to sustain capitalist development. While insisting on cultural and historical specificity, Asian feminist theologians cannot indulge in narrow nationalism, identity politics
and ethnic separatism, all of which pit one group against the other,
creating a climate of competition in which each group claims to be the
most victimized. Instead, they must constantly seek ways to form coali-

tions among women and to strengthen solidarity across national, cultural, economic, and religious boundaries. Speaking on women in solidarity with women, Elizabeth Tapia explains the need for solidarity as follows:

> We need to be in solidarity with one another to counteract feelings, and forces of separation, competition, and powerlessness…
>
> We need to be in solidarity with each other because of the heavy dose of patriarchy, which includes sexism, racism, and classism.
>
> We need to be in solidarity to enjoy friendships and affirm differences as well as God-given gifts.
>
> We need to be in solidarity with the victims of domestic and sexual violence.
>
> We need to be in solidarity with the poor, who are victims of economic injustice (Tapia 1992: 27).

Chapter 3

Sources and Resources of Asian Feminist Theology

Asian women theologians should realize that *we are the text*, and the Bible and tradition of the Christian church are the context of our theology.

Chung Hyun Kyung (Korea)

To articulate feminist theology from a cultural matrix that is so ancient, multistranded and deeply spiritual is an awesome task. Trying to find a new language for theology, Asian feminist theologians know that they have to reconnect with their Asian roots and spirituality. As one Asian poem indicates:

Asia…
We pause in silence
Before the awesome reality of Asia.
Her vastness, variety and complexity,
Her peoples, languages, cultures,
The richness of her history
And the present poverty of her peoples.
We take Asia to our hearts,
See her and feel her within us,
Embrace her
In her wholeness and brokenness,
While her rivers and tears flow through us,
Her winds, her sighs, her spirits,
Her moans, her howls blow within us (Fabella, Lee and Suh 1992: 148).

To embark on this journey, Asian feminist theologians look for new sources, symbols, images and stories that help them to articulate their experiences of God. They re-examine the colonial and patriarchal inter-pretations of the Bible and search for liberating elements for their pre-sent struggles. As Christians, they live in an enchanting world of gods and goddesses with colorful religious rituals and many alternative forms of spirituality. In this chapter, I shall analyze critical issues that have emerged in Asian women's discussion about the sources and resources of their theology: the use of women's experience in theology, the liberation of the Bible from colonial bondage, and the critical appropriation of Asian religious traditions.

Asian Women's Experience: Commonality and Diversity

Asian feminist theologians argue that they have to do their own theology because their experiences have been left out of theological reflection. But women's experience is a contested source of feminist theology. Feminist theologians in the past two decades have debated on what constitutes women's experience and how experience, given its diverse and changing nature, can be normative in theology. Theologian Rebecca Chopp distinguishes two alternative epistemological approaches based on women's experiences: standpoint theory and social constructionism (Chopp 1996: 116-23). Those who choose to follow standpoint theory argue that women's knowing is ontologically different from men's, and some even advocate that women know more about love, relationships and God. People who have suffered under colonialism will see immediately the fallacy of this romantic view of women's nature because their colonizers have been both male and female. Female colonizers, either through their overt support of the colonial regime or through their silent complicity, have not demonstrated themselves to know more about loving and God.

The social constructionist approach, according to Chopp, posits that 'knowledge is itself always historical, always related to power and interests, and is open to change and transformation' (Chopp 1996: 120). Feminist theologians who support this position refuse to universalize women's experience and stress instead the diversity of these experiences. Since women's experience is always shaped by a complex interaction of factors, such as class, race, colonialism and sexual orientation, a woman's viewpoint will always reflect her situation and perspective. The emphasis on the historical character of knowledge and human experience offers more room for feminist theologians to dialogue across differences and for multiply oppressed women to articulate diverse theological voices.

When we talk about 'women's experiences' in China or Pakistan, let alone 'women's experiences' in *Asia* generally, we are always talking about a social construct. To understand how women construct and express their experiences in different parts of Asia, feminist theologians rely on story-telling and social analysis, as well as the poetry, art, symbols and rituals created by women. Story-telling has been the chief means of passing wisdom from one generation of women to another, as most Asian women have been illiterate until recent times. The story of the 'comfort women', for example, has served as a 'root story' for many Korean feminist theologians to elucidate the intersection of colonialism, militarism and sexism. Critical social analysis is necessary to examine the systemic oppression that exists in political, economic, social and cultural realms. It is especially significant today when the interlocking mechanism of globalization oppresses millions of people, without people even being aware of it. Asian women's religious lives are richly expressed through the symbolism of color, sound and image (Rebera 1990). When Asian women theologians meet, they have always celebrated their lives and God's gifts through rituals. Many of these innovative and moving rituals can be found on the pages of the journal *In God's Image*.

When Asian feminist theology first emerged in the late 1970s, theologians tended to stress the commonalities of Asian women's experience. Except for women in Japan and in Thailand, the majority of women in Asia have the shared experience of emerging from a long history of colonialism. After World War II, Asian countries were poor and in the early stages of economic development. Except for the Philippines, most Asian Christian communities are tiny minorities, having to compete for existence with the numerous other religious traditions in Asia. The male-dominated church structures are often reinforced by the patriarchal elements of indigenous culture. Furthermore, when the theological current was so fresh and new, these women theologians saw the need to come together and express solidarity with one another. Many had just learned to embrace their *Asian* identity with joy and pride, and they wanted to differentiate their feminist theology from that being developed by Western women at the same time. Some of the feminist theologians were able to meet other Asian women for the first time, and they wanted to identify common issues so they could work together.

While it may have been strategically important to stress commonalities in the earlier period, in the 1990s Asian feminist theologians have called for more attention to the diversity of women's experiences. Kang Nam-Soon of Korea has cautioned against the strong tendencies of universalization and oversimplification in constructing and presenting Asian women's theology. She writes:

Asian feminist theologians, despite certain common cultural bases, have extremely diverse histories, religions, cultures and traditions. Sharing a common goal to end primarily patriarchal domination does not prevent feminist theologians from having radically divergent perspectives on how that goal might be reached (Kang 1995: 22).

Just as white, middle-class feminists should not generalize their experiences, Asian feminist theologians should guard against presenting a monolithic, simplified notion of what it means to be 'Asian'. Angela Wong Wai Ching of Hong Kong has observed that Asian women have been portrayed stereotypically as either victims or heroic women who take part in national struggles and other forms of liberation. Such polar constructs oversimplify Asian women's experience and blur their different localities such as ethnic groups, class, history and culture. Many women will not fit in a stereotypical, generalized, and ahistorical image of the 'Asian woman' (Ching 1999).

To accentuate their diversity, Asian feminist theologians must pay acute attention to the issue of economic disparity among women, both regionally and nationally. The widening gap between the richer and poorer countries in Asia affects women's standard of living and levels of economic independence. In addition to Japanese conglomerates, Korean and Taiwanese companies are setting up multinational corporations in many parts of the world. Feminists in East Asia can no longer claim to be economically oppressed, without recognizing that they have the potential to benefit from a global system that oppresses many others. They have to theologize from the perspective of both the oppressed and the oppressor at the same time. Moreover, the accumulation of capital within a small sector of society and the increased demand for highly skilled workers result in the acutely uneven distribution of wealth within a country. A professional woman in Seoul earns several times more than an unskilled female worker. A woman who owns a small business in the Special Economic Zone in China enjoys a much more comfortable life than a rural woman in the hinterland.

Feminist theology in Asia has largely been a middle-class movement, just as it has been in many other parts of the world. It has been developed by educated, middle-class ministers, church workers, academics, religious women and community organizers. As a movement, it faces challenges from many sides. First, feminist theology has not sufficiently impacted the theological discourse and the structures of patriarchal churches. Second, many women sitting in the pews have not heard about feminist theology, and many would consider feminism to be too radical and aggressive. Third, as middle-class women, many Asian feminist theologians have yet to find ways to join with the efforts of uneducated and lower-class women in order to bring about societal transformation. They have to be very conscious that their theological imagination is limited by their horizons, and they should not claim to represent or speak for all Asian women.

Besides economic disparity, Asian women's diverse experiences are also shaped by such factors as ethnicity, caste, sexual orientation and migration. The better-known feminist theologians from Asia all come from the dominant ethnic groups in their countries. But women belonging to minorities and indigenous groups exist in many parts of Asia, being marginalized in more than one way. For example, there are tribal indigenous women in Taiwan, minority Korean women in Japan, and minority Tamil women in Sri Lanka. In India, women face discrimination, not only because of gender, but also because of clan and caste. The voices of dalit women have just recently been heard in ecumenical circles. Dalits are the untouchables who belong to the lowest caste. In Hong Kong, India, and in other parts of Asia, lesbians have begun to organize themselves, but female homosexuality is still a taboo subject in public discourse. The number of migrant female workers continues to increase, and they are now working not only in other Asian countries, but also in the Middle East. The theological aspirations derived from their experiences of diaspora have scarcely been told.

In order to become a mature theological movement, Asian feminist theology needs to diversify, and to continue to bring in new voices. There should be different theoretical frameworks and models for doing theology. Mutual criticism and constructive dialogues among women of different social locations should be fostered. Creative ways of networking, innovative communicative styles, and genuine community-building that facilitates the participation of grassroots women should be explored in the future.

The Bible: Bread Or Stone?

In the past several decades, feminist theologians and biblical scholars have made significant contributions to recovering the Bible as bread rather than stone for women. Using the critical lens of a hermeneutics of suspicion, feminist scholarship has critiqued many traditional claims regarding the Bible. Feminist theologians have challenged the authority of the Bible, the boundary of the canon and the androcentric bias of both the text and the history of interpretation. Seeking to construct feminist models of interpretation, they have scrutinized the master's tools, created feminist frames of meaning, and developed different norms of interpretation. Reconstructing women's early Christian history, they examined the everyday lives of women, women's religious leadership in church and synagogue and the marginalization of women in the patriarchalization of the church. They proposed new liturgical usage of the Bible, alternative methods of feminist Bible study, and liberating paradigms for teaching biblical studies. (For a helpful guide to the breadth of feminist scholarship on the Bible, see Schüssler Fiorenza 1993).

These issues are significant for women in diverse contexts. Throughout the past decade, feminist scholars from the Third World and from minority communities in the United States have increasingly contributed to the emerging feminist biblical scholarship. In the case of the Asian situation, we need to discuss a few issues before the Bible can be used as a resource for Asian feminist theology: the use of the Bible in colonial discourse, the influence of colonialism in the academic study of the Bible and the possibilities of developing feminist postcolonial readings of the Bible.

The Bible is an integral part of the colonial discourse. The introduction of the Bible and Christian faith to foreign lands was used to justify the political and military aggression of the West. For example, Hong Kong was ceded to the British in 1842 in the same unequal treaty that granted missionaries permission to preach in the seaports of China. To teach the Bible and to spread the Gospel were seen as the 'civilizing mission' of the West, or as the 'white man's burden'. For example one missionary in China declared that: 'The great civilizing agent of the world is the Holy Scripture' (Porter 1890: 294). Selected passages from the Bible were emphasized to justify this cause. For example, the Great Commission of Jesus to go and make disciples of all nations (Mt. 28.19) was given unprecedented attention during the colonization of India by missionaries (Sugirtharajah 1998b: 95).

Revered as the revealed Word of God, the Bible was seen as the prize possession of the West. The Bible thus served as a 'signifier' that functioned to support Western beliefs in the inferiority and deficiency of 'heathen' cultures. Furthermore, revelation through the Bible was regarded as special revelation. Insights and wisdom offered by other religions and traditions could at best be classified as general revelation. This biased view reinforced the superiority of Christianity in the evolutionary scheme of religion, developed in the nineteenth century to justify colonialism.

The introduction of the Bible to other cultures was a mixed blessing for women. In order to teach women to read the Bible, Christian missions established girls' schools, catechism classes and women's Bible study classes. While the provision of female education helped to promote literacy, the curriculum of these mission girls' schools was meant to instill the cult of true womanhood and to reinforce domesticity of women (see Kwok 1992: 104-106). The requirement of knowledge of the Bible for baptism required the training of Bible women and female evangelists to teach the illiterate women to read. These female church workers often functioned as teacher, social worker and counselor in their local communities. The segregation of the sexes called for the sending of female missionaries, who often displayed ethnocentrism toward their 'heathen' sisters, but also provided role models for women.

While the enthnocentrism of missionaries working 'in the frontiers' has been criticized, the academics studying the Bible in the metropolitan centers of Europe were seen as immune from cultural imperialism. Little reflection has been done on the relationship between the emergence of the historical critical method and the ascendency of European power. There are two reasons for this oversight: First, in the West the historical critical method has been seen as a progressive tool to challenge church dogma and the authority of the church. Second, the method was considered by its practitioners as scientific, objective and value-neutral. Focusing on the bygone era of the Greco-Roman world, historical critical research was not supposed to be clouded by the political interests of the time.

However, if we examine historical criticism from an international point of view, a different picture begins to emerge. We can cite as an example the first quest for the historical Jesus, a paramount concern of historical criticism (for details see Kwok 1998: 69-85). Some of the key spokespersons of the first quest were not disinterested scholars, but defenders of national power and the supremacy of European culture. D.F. Strauss (1808–1874), a supporter of a strong and united Germany under the hegemony of Prussia, defended Germany's position in the Prusso-Austrian war. Ernest Renan (1823–92), who was passionate about French high culture, went to Phoenicia and Syria under the auspices of

Napoleon III. An interpreter of Bach's organ music, Albert Schweitzer (1875–1965) left us not only a *summa* of the first quest but also an auto-biography detailing his life as a 'jungle doctor'. Labeling African people as 'primitive creatures' without much progress, his autobiography dis-played deep-seated feelings of cultural superiority.

The incursions of Europeans into other parts of the world affected these scholars' conceptualization of both Western civilization and Chris-tianity. The nineteenth-century comparative study of myths and religions proposed an interpretation of 'primitive' peoples as mythical, supersti-tious and idolatrous. To prove that Christianity was infinitely superior to other religions, all the nonsense of virgin birth, miracles and super-natural happenings surrounding Jesus had to be discarded. This could only be done by a 'critical' or 'scientific' study of the Bible, which would uncover an historical Jesus free of any mythological trappings. The quest for the historical Jesus was far from being value-neutral. The political interests of Europe determined the questions to be asked, the gathering of data, the framework of interpretation and the final out-come.

The historical critical method must be situated within the cultural space and political configurations of its time. We must begin to question its assumptions about historical consciousness, historicity and historiog-raphy from a postcolonial perspective. The historical questions raised by this method may be too limiting for people in other contexts. In fact, other cultures have other assumptions about history and their own historical method. For example, the Chinese have always studied history not so much for 'objective' data as for insights to illuminate the present. The Indians value the myths and stories that have shaped their under-standing of their ancient past. A *Western* historical criticism should not be taken as universally valid because *Western* notions of historical process are not universally held. We have to learn from the insights of other cultures to broaden our historical imagination.

The discussion of the postcolonial interpretation of the Bible has gained momentum among Third World scholars and intellectuals within the indigenous and diasporic communities. R.S. Sugirtharajah has said that the postcolonial perspective will have to go beyond a mimicry of Western critical method and an Orientalist valorization of ancient pre-colonial cultures (Sugirtharajah 1998a). It has to negotiate a different past, one that has not been reified, glorified and seen as unitary. Em-ploying tools from critical theory and cultural studies, postcolonial criticism exposes the relationship between power and knowledge, challenges both imperialist and nationalist claims, and maintains the posture of a 'fighting literature'.

There are several characteristics of postcolonial criticism: (1) it challenges the universalizing forms of Western interpretation, exposing its co-optation by imperial interests and destabilizing its frames of meaning; (2) it is a counterhegemonic discourse, paying special attention to the hidden and neglected voices in the Bible; (3) it places the Bible within the multifaith context of many Third World situations; (4) it encourages and welcomes contributions from marginalized groups that have not been fully heard: the dalits, indigenous peoples, migrants, people in diaspora and in borderlands, especially the women in these communities; (5) it learns from and debates with other hermeneutical frameworks, such as postmodernism.

Insights from postcolonial discourse have recently been introduced to Asian feminist biblical criticism. In the past, Asian feminist theologians who were theologically trained often relied on biblical scholarship from North America (e.g. Gnanadason 1988: 44-51; Park 1987: 66-75). The works of Elisabeth Schüssler Fiorenza, Rosemary Radford Ruether and Phyllis Trible were introduced or translated into the Asian languages. It was assumed that these scholars would tell us what the Bible meant and that their findings could be correlated with Asian women's experiences. But Asian feminist theologians had become more aware that all feminist interpretations are context-bound. There is no 'value-neutral' feminist interpretation that is applicable to all contexts, and Asian feminists have to find their own principles of interpretation.

Postcolonial feminist criticism from Asia should examine the Bible from the vantage point of women multiply oppressed because of race, class, militarism and colonialism. It investigates how marginalized women in the Bible are rendered invisible, consigned to signify the Other and denied a voice of their own. At the same time, it reconstructs the lives of these women and plots a subversive feminist discourse based on fragments and traces that are still left in the biblical tradition. Instead of focusing on the activities of female leaders in the church as other feminist scholars have done, it seeks to illuminate the everyday lives of ordinary women. The lives and struggles of Jewish women under the foreign rules of Babylon, Persia, the Greeks and the Romans should be of great interest to contemporary postcolonial critics. And rather than constantly looking to the West for insights, Asian feminist biblical scholars can learn much from feminist scholarship from the Third World and from minorities in North America. In the next chapter I shall discuss in more detail feminist interpretations of the Bible from Asia in recent years.

Asian Religious Traditions: Blessing and Curse

Western feminist theologians have criticized the androcentric symbolism and teachings of Christianity as reinforcing male domination in society. Mary Daly has claimed that 'if God is male, then the male is God' (Daly 1973: 19). Likewise in Asia it is the Asian religious traditions that have been blamed for undergirding the millennia-old sexual discrimination against women. The first Asian Women's Consultation on Interfaith Dialogue brought together 35 women and men from 17 countries in the Asia–Pacific region. The report of the conference states that the original teachings of many of the world's religions were both inclusive and liberative of the human person. But the distortions of these teachings have led to discriminatory laws and religious practices against women, the limitation of women's leadership and ritualistic roles, and the denigration of women's bodies as unclean and polluting. It concludes that:

> As a result of this religious discrimination, women of all religions continue to be marginalized and discriminated against at the societal level. Traditional practices, which have religious overtones include the purdah system, female genital mutilation, polygamy, silencing of women. The demand for virginity and chastity only from women has led to miserable womanhood and widowhood.[1]

Although many Asian feminist theologians are critical of the discriminatory practices of Asian religions, they also look for liberating aspects in which women may have played more significant roles. For example, Korean feminists have emphasized the influences of shamanism on women's spirituality, and the important role of the female shaman in local communities. Filipino feminists point to a more egalitarian social structure and the higher status of women within their indigenous traditions during precolonial times as compared to Filipino women's experiences under Roman Catholicism. Others have pointed to the rich

1. 'Summary Report of the First Asian Women's Consultation on Inter-faith Dialogue, November 1-8, 1989, Kuala Lumpur, Malaysia', *In God's Image* (December 1989), p. 5.

traditions of feminine symbolism in Hinduism, the establishment of nunneries as an alternative to patriarchal family in Buddhism and the Islamic belief in human equality as liberative elements.

Asian feminist theologians have moved away from the simple caricature that Asian religious traditions are either blessing or curse for women. But much more critical scrutiny and scholarly work on these traditions are needed in the future so that they can offer insights and resources for feminist theological thinking. First, feminist study of Asian religious traditions has to go beyond cataloguing blatantly discriminatory texts to an investigation of how such texts function in their respective historical contexts. For example, Asian feminists can easily find the Confucian injunction of the three obediences required of women: to obey her father before marriage, her husband after marriage, and her son when widowed, or the teachings that women should be subordinate in the Upanishads and Vedas (EATWOT 1994: 93-98, 99-105). But attention should be paid to the circumstances within which these teachings emerged and to what extent they were practiced. Feminist scholars of the Bible have long pointed out that biblical texts reflect the male author's point of view and may not reflect the reality of women's lives. Further, Asian texts may have performed particular rhetorical functions to persuade people and served special ideological purposes at their time. Given the fact that most Asian religions have long, complex, pluralistic and multilayered histories, a careful study of women's situations in various historical epochs is necessary. Buddhist, Confucian, Islamic and Hindu views of women certainly have changed over time, and women's relationship with these traditions has never been monolithic, but rather dependent on women's educational attainment, social status, and sometimes geographical locale.

The study of the influences of Asian religions on women should also be cross-cultural. For example, classical Confucian teaching, originating with Confucius (551–479 BCE), may not have included extremely restrictive and derogatory views of women. But Neo-Confucianism, which emerged between the tenth and the twelfth centuries, promulgated a stricter code of sexual conduct for women. Chastity became an utmost virtue for women, and widows were discouraged from remarriage. It was Neo-Confucianism that was introduced to Korea during the Yi Dynasty (1392–1910), and which soon became political ideology to control Korean people and to subdue women. Ever since China encountered the military and technological strength of the West, beginning in the mid-nineteenth century, there have been serious critiques of Confucianism, especially during the Cultural Revolution (1966–76). Since the 1920s radical intellectuals, insisting that China should be thoroughly Westernized, have condemned Confucianism as feudalistic, backward-looking and even patriarchal. But the Confucian ideology in Korea has not gone through such in-depth and wholesale criticism and its grip on the Korean people is still strong. Today, Korean women may feel the impact of Confucianism more than women in socialist China, Westernized Hong Kong and a politically transformed Taiwan. A cross-cultural comparison of how Confucianism has influenced gender construction in different societies and during varied historical periods will help Asian feminists to understand in a nuanced way the religious and cultural legitimation of patriarchy. Similar cross-cultural study can also be done for Asian religious traditions, such as Hinduism, Buddhism, Daoism and Shinto. At the second Interfaith Conference from Asian Women's Perspectives held in 1991, some comparative work was done on Confucianism in Taiwan and Korea. At the same time, scholars from Japan, Thailand and Sri Lanka presented papers on Buddhism and women in their own cultural contexts.

Asian feminist theologians must also promote a tradition of feminist scholarship on Asian religious traditions. Currently most of the scholarship on Asian religions is done by Asian men, who do not pay much attention to women's issues. A lot of feminist scholarship on Asian religions derives from Western female scholars in the academy of North America, some of whom are converts to these religions (see Gross 1996). On the one hand, some of them display ethnocentric attitudes toward Asian traditions, regarding Asian women as victims of strange and bizarre religious beliefs and social practices. Some years ago there was quite a debate among feminists in North America regarding how to interpret sati in India, the custom of widows burning alive on their husbands' funeral pyres. On the other hand, some new converts tend to have romantic feelings about their new religion and focus on more positive or transformative aspects of the tradition. For example the existence of a plurality of goddesses in Buddhism and Hinduism has been taken out of context in Western women's search for the feminine dimension of the divine. It is unfortunate that few Asian women are trained in the field of religious studies, or specialize in the study of their own religious traditions. Very often we have Christian Asian women commenting on or critiquing Buddhism, Confucianism or Hinduism. Such imbalance in scholarship may produce skewed or biased pictures of women's lives within the complex and pluralistic religious worlds of Asia.

Finally, we need to address the question of whether there are limits, or parameters, for Asian feminist theologians to appropriate religious resources from their cultures. Some Asian feminist theologians have found that the model of interreligious dialogue in the ecumenical movement is not adequate in some situations. Within this model, believers of different religions enter into critical conversations with one another, and each is transformed in the dialogical process. But in Asia, the boundaries of religions are not clear cut: one can be a Shinto and a Buddhist in Japan, or a Christian who consults shamans during a crisis in Korea or a Confucian-Buddhist in Malaysia. Religious identity is not constructed in a uniform way and the term *religion* has its origin in the West. Chung Hyun Kyung has called this multifaith dialogue within oneself intra-religious dialogue. In fact, Christianity has always been a cultural hybrid since it was 'translated' in Asia. The Chinese Bible, for example, was translated by the missionaries into the Chinese language, using many terminologies from Buddhism. Indigenous images, symbols and religious practices have been adopted to help evangelize the Gospel.

On the other hand, Asian feminist theologians should guard against indiscriminate appropriation and mindless borrowing. There is a fine line between discerning theological significance in indigenous religious resources and simply baptizing other traditions or integrating them within the Christian narrative. The latter can result in a diluted form of Christian imperialism, lacking respect for the integrity of the tradition concerned. Asian feminist theologians can learn from the long history of mixing and blending different religious traditions in their context to generate principles and guidelines for critical appropriation of indigenous resources. Since the Asian feminist theological movement is so new, there is much room for experimentation and risk-taking. Mutual criticism and openness to the critique of women of other faith traditions is essential. Such critical engagement with one another is necessary if women of all faith traditions are to work together for the liberation and well-being of all women.

Chapter Four

Asian Feminist Interpretations of the Bible

Today we must claim back the power to look at the Bible with our own
eyes and to stress that divine immanence is within us, not in something
sealed off and handed down from almost two thousand years ago.

Kwok Pui-lan (Hong Kong)

Asian feminist theology began with small groups of women reading
the Bible and relating it to their realities and their struggles in everyday
life. The Bible has a central role in Asian churches and plays a significant
part in women's spirituality because of the strong Protestant evangelical
heritage in Asia. Asian feminist theologians have emphasized the need to
reinterpret the Bible so that it could not be used as a tool to oppress
women. Innovative Bible studies have been promoted in women's
Christian fellowships and ecumenical gatherings to encourage women to
look at the Bible through a liberating lens. Searching for critical principles of interpretation, different theological networks of Asian feminist
theologians have organized seminars and workshops on biblical hermeneutics and published books and anthologies on the subject.

Most proponents of the feminist study of the Bible in Asia have
received some theological training, but they are not professional biblical
scholars. Their reflections on the Bible are meant to stimulate feminist
consciousness among church women in a pastoral context, instead of
targeting an academic audience. The styles of these Bible studies display
great variety and creativity: story-telling, dialogues, poetry, drama, skits
and performance. Although feminist hermeneutics is still quite new in
Asia, several different approaches to the Bible can be identified. These
approaches are not mutually exclusive, the boundaries between them
being quite fluid.

Women's Heritage in the Bible

The first model of feminist hermeneutics aims to recover the memory of women in the Bible to serve as role models, since the Asian, male-dominated churches tend to undermine their significance. Several prominent women in the Hebrew Scriptures are noted for their faith in God and courageous acts. For example, a group of Asian women found that Naomi and Ruth were extraordinarily confident and courageous women, who participated actively in shaping their own destiny. In sharp contrast, the images of women conveyed from the pulpits are often gentle, submissive and obedient. In the book of Ruth, they observed that 'the image of woman that comes to us is one in which two women, faced by very difficult situations indeed, through their faith challenge both the power structures of their times as well as create new personal meanings' (Ng 1982: 9). Another favorite figure that is often cited is Hannah, who was discriminated against because she was barren. Many Asian women in similar situations sympathize with her because to produce a son is still an important obligation for wives in Asia. Calling Hannah a role model, Esther Inayat of Pakistan praises her for her steadfast faith and her prayer (Inayat 1992: 85-92). The promise of God to Hannah offers hope and solace for desperate women in similar situations. The story of Miriam also inspires Asian women. A prophetess like Deborah, she was chosen by God to lead the Israelites out of bondage (Inayat 1988: 29-30).

More emphasis, however, is on women in the New Testament, especially the women in the life and ministry of Jesus. Reflections on Mary, the mother of Jesus, feature prominently in Bible studies written by women, especially among Roman Catholics. Mary is not seen as a subservient and gentle maiden, but is hailed as a prototype of full womanhood. Her virginity is interpreted as the freedom to serve God and not be subject to any other human being. As the mother of the savior, Mary is a giver of life and co-redeemer. But Mary is not only a virgin and a mother, she is also a true disciple. She ponders God's word in her heart and responds to God's challenge with courage and determination (Chung 1990: 74-84). Besides Mary, women followers of Jesus, particularly those who were present at his death and witnessed his resurrection, are remembered fondly as workers for God's mission during a critical point in history (Chang 1986: 46-47). In addition, the Samaritan woman whom Jesus met at the well and engaged in conversation is credited for propagating the good news; and the Syrophoenician woman, for breaking social taboos to seek help from Jesus to heal her daughter.

This approach shows that biblical women can be exemplars for today's Asian women by underscoring their participation in God's mission and their contributions to history. The authority of the Bible is not questioned. In fact, the stories of strong and courageous women in the Bible are used to sanction Asian women's contemporary struggle for equality. This approach has strong appeal for those Asian Christian women who regard the Bible as the Word of God and who have been brought up to read the Bible quite literally. The Bible is not seen as a problem for women. Its message is basically liberating if we do not read it from a biased male perspective.

The difficulty with this approach is that the roles the women in the Bible played were often circumscribed by the male-dominated society. Many of these women were associated with male heroes. For example, Miriam played an auxiliary role to Moses and Aaron, and Hannah was finally able to produce a male heir to continue the patrilineal heritage. The cataloguing of strong women in the Bible has been done with a remedial agenda, without fully integrating these women into the patriarchal history and culture. Moreover, in trying to rescue the Bible, this approach fails to pay sufficient attention to the pervasive portrayal of women as property, as whores and as victims of society. Some writers emphasize Jesus' liberating attitudes toward women in contrast to the Jewish customs of the time. Such an interpretation has been criticized as serving the apologetic interests of Christians, which might contribute to anti-Semitism.

Oral Interpretation and Re-telling of Biblical Stories

In many Asian cultures, the scriptures have been chanted, recited, memorized and performed for millennia because the spoken words are considered more sacred than the written texts. A comparative study of the function of scripture in the world's religions has shown that oral transmission of scripture has been the dominant mode in many traditions. Even in the West, silent reading of the written text of the Bible became important only after popular education and printing became affordable. For many Asian Christian women, Bible studies mean gathering together to talk about the biblical stories and relating them to their everyday lives.

Anthropologists, such as Jack Goody, have pointed out that oral interpretation has its own logic, quite different from that employed to interpret written texts. For example, oral transmission and interpretation often have a more fluid understanding of the boundaries of the 'text'. The same story can be told in many different ways, depending on the situation and the response of the audience. In re-telling the 'text', the interpreter is not interested primarily in what happened in the past, but in how the story can be brought alive for the present. Oral interpretation can potentially be more participatory and democratic, since illiterate and uneducated people can share their point of view as well. The accent on orality in Asian traditions further challenges the hierarchal notion that written and literate cultures are more sophisticated and advanced. It underscores the fact that in many settings, there is an interplay between the oral and the written, that the oral text and the written text exist in a continuum.

One of the strategies of oral interpretation is to give voice to women in the Bible and to recreate their dialogues. For example, in a re-telling of the story of Moses' birth by a group of Asian women, the Hebrew midwives Shiprah and Puah discuss with Jochebed (Moses' mother) and another mother, Susannah, how they managed to save the baby Moses:

Shiprah:	We told Pharaoh that the Hebrew women are so strong that they delivered their babies before we arrived to assist.
Jochebed:	Praise God for giving you wisdom.
Susannah:	You were not treated badly, were you?
Puah:	Pharaoh's men kicked us and threatened to kill us if we would not follow Pharaoh's command.
Jochebed:	The power of Yahweh be with you and protect you (John *et al.* 1988: 45).

Another commonly used strategy is the re-telling of biblical stories from women's perspective, using a woman as the narrator. Pauline Hensman of Sri Lanka re-tells the life and death of Jesus through the eyes of Mary. She begins her Gospel according to Mary by saying:

Dear Sisters: My son also suffered a horrible death. He was tortured and killed. It took me a long time to understand why a good man like him had to die. Perhaps it will help you also to understand if I tell you about him (Hensman 1985: 24).

In addition to the narrative form, sometimes poetry, drama, skits, dance, mime and pictures are used. In a moving poem that recasts the story of the bent-over woman (Lk. 13.10-17), Dulcie Abraham of Malaysia writes:

They said he makes the blind to see,
And heals the lame,
Ah, why not me?

I know I was not meant
To spend my life thus bent
In pain's unending captivity.

A bent woman—they looked away
But secret longings to be free
Led me to him to seek release.

On the crowd's edge I found a place
I could not see his face, but stood.
My back bent low, to hear his word.

Then suddenly I heard him call:
He spoke to me:
'Woman, I set you free,
from your bondage and infirmity!'

His hands reached out and straightened me,
The world spun round—I looked to find
My Savior—but he was gone…

And I was straight and whole—
I praised my God with joyful heart
That God had set me free!

One day when months had passed
I saw my Savior—now he was BENT
Beneath a heavy tree…

'Weep not for me', he said,
And as I wept I knew it was to set me free
My Savior was bent beneath that heavy tree (Abraham 1986: 78).

These feminist re-tellings of the biblical stories reclaim women as subjects with their own thoughts, feelings and voice. The new stories expand the imagination of the members in the audience and enable them to identify easily with the female characters. Since Asian cultures are so different from that of the biblical context, the re-telling can bridge the gap created by space and time. There is no limit as to how the story can be recast as the interpreter is not limited by a fixed written text. The stories of the Bible are valued as depositories of religious and moral insights, rather than historical records of what happened in the past.

But not all oral re-telling is liberating. The stories can also be told using the androcentric framework provided by the biblical text, as many male pastors have done. Since one of the expressed goals of oral interpretation is to make the text relevant to the present, the audiences must participate in defining what kind of interpretation is liberating for them. The critical norm of interpretation cannot be provided by the storyteller or the audience alone, but in the dialogical process between the two. The laity, especially women sitting in the pew, should be encouraged to participate in the critical evaluative process. Oral transmission and interpretation has so far received little scholarly scrutiny in Asian academic circles. I hope Asian feminist theologians will develop more guidelines and principles for this work in the near future.

A Socio-Political Reading

Asian feminist theologians are able to demonstrate the relevance of the Bible to contemporary settings by reading it within the frame of present socio-political struggles. The urgent questions of today determine what passages or themes of the Bible are significant and also the method of interpretation. These theologians have found that ancient Israel's efforts to survive in the midst of strong neighboring nations have close parallels in contemporary Asian politics. Women living in a multi-ethnic society find the issues of religion and politics, economic justice, and harmony and conflict as relevant today as in biblical times.

Korea is one of the countries that remains divided after World War II, and the theme of reunification remains central in Korean feminist theology. Lee Oo Chung, one of the pioneers of feminist theology in Korea, has led several bible studies on the themes of peace and unification in the Bible. Expounding on Eph. 2.14-18, she shows that peace and unification are central to the message of salvation. Through reconciliation in Christ, 'the dividing wall set up by enmity is broken down, and the divided community is made one through reconciliation with one another' (Lee 1988: 25). She emphasizes the theme of peace as especially relevant in the Korean situation, where brothers and sisters have killed each other in the Korean War (1950–53), and where animosity has continued to grow ever since the division of the country.

In another study of the concept of Shalom in the Hebrew Scriptures,

Lee Oo Chung suggests that the origin of peace lies in God, rooted in God's righteousness and justice (Lee 1992: 193-204). *Shalom*, as Lee points out, has multiple meanings: a state of well-being, health and safety, the absence of war, prosperity, and dwelling in security without threat from neighbors. Like the false prophets who proclaimed peace when there was no peace, politicians and bureaucrats in Korea have misused the word peace to hide an unjust political and economic situation. In the name of maintaining peace and the security of the peninsula, South Korea has become one of the most militarized zones in the world. Lee condemns this use of *peace* as part of an ideology that serves to manipulate and oppress people. For her, Micah's eschatological vision depicting the realization of true peace is as relevant today as in his time: 'they shall beat their swords into plowshares, and their spears into pruning hooks; nation shall not lift up sword against nation, neither shall they learn war any more' (Mic. 4.3).

In other Asian contexts where ethnic strife has ripped communities apart, lessons are drawn from stories about human relationship among different racial and ethnic groups in the Bible. In the beautiful country of Sri Lanka, the majority group of Singhalese and the Tamils, who are in the minority, have been fighting with each other for more than a decade. Chitra Fernando of Sri Lanka has reflected on the theme of women and racism in the Bible. Focusing on the story of Sarah and Hagar, she points out that Hagar was discriminated against because she belonged to another race. Yet, the story also shows that God responded to the needs of Hagar and her child, offering them protection in the wilderness. In today's context, Fernando stresses, God likewise hears the cries of mothers for their children, who are made to suffer on account of racism and other forms of bigotry. She praises the work of the Women for Peace Movement in Sri Lanka, where mothers of the north and mothers of the south join together to express a common concern regarding the lives of their husbands and children in the midst of present ethnic violence (Fernando 1986: 43). For Fernando, the story of Ruth is another biblical narrative that offers insights for overcoming racial prejudice and transcending ethnic boundaries. The Moabite Ruth had such great love and respect for her Jewish mother-in-law, Naomi, that she was willing to follow her and live among her people. Ruth's selfless devotion to her mother-in-law challenged Boaz to respond in a similar fashion. When a son was born to Ruth and Boaz, the women of Jeru-

salem overcame their prejudice in acclaiming that Ruth the Moabitess
was 'better than seven sons' (Fernando 1986: 44).

From the Japanese context, Hisako Kinukawa has developed a sociological and rhetorical approach to the Bible that combines her training
in Western biblical scholarship with feminist insights. In her *Women and
Jesus in Mark*, she shows how this approach helps her to reread stories of
women in Mark's Gospel. Her method is sociological because she pays
attention to the sociological and anthropological analysis of the society
that shaped Mark's narrative. Borrowing insights from Bruce Malina's
anthropological study of the Bible, she shows how a value system built
on honor and shame, the dyadic personality (people who depend upon
the opinions and evaluations of others), and the unequal sexual status
between men and women that prevailed in the ancient Mediterranean
world also operates in her Japanese society:

> As a woman, I can feel closer to the women in the Bible, since our
> experiences as women have so much in common with theirs. Such com-
> mon experiences of shame/honor with boundaries of power, sexual status,
> and respect for others, in a group-oriented society of dyadic personalities,
> provide me with a powerful methodological device for studying the
> women and their experiences in Mark's Gospel (Kinukawa 1994: 16).

But Kinukawa's approach also uses methodological insights that
derived from critical rhetorical studies, especially from the works of
Elisabeth Schüssler Fiorenza and Antoinette Clark Wire. Kinukawa
stresses that biblical texts are not data for historical reconstruction. On
the contrary, they are expressive discourses reflecting the symbolic
worlds out of which they come. Rhetorical criticism pays attention to
the rhetorical function and persuasive power of the text. Mark's Gospel
was written with an intention to shape a certain worldview and to
motivate the audience to respond and act in a certain way. Any interpreter must critically evaluate the public character and function of the
text in its political, social and religious roles. At the same time, she must
keep in mind that contemporary interpretations also have political
responsibility in shaping the ethos of the faith community (Kinukawa
1994: 22-28).

I shall cite her discussion of the hemorrhaging woman (Mk 5.25-34)
to illustrate her method. (The discussion below is based on Kinukawa
1994: 29-50). The hemorrhaging woman suffered from patriarchal discrimination reinforced by religious ideology because she would have

not only been considered sick, but polluted as well. While the patriarchy of first-century Judaea was reinforced by faith in the God, Yahweh, patriarchy in Japan is legitimized by emperor worship and the religious teachings of Shinto, Confucianism, Buddhism and Christianity. These various traditions combine to keep women in bondage through purity codes, filial piety and religious precepts. For example, according to Shinto belief, women are considered polluted during menstruation and the time around childbirth, and should not enter Shinto shrines during those periods.

Following the purity laws in Leviticus, the hemorrhaging woman would have been an outcast, 'polluted'. Those who were polluted were segregated from society in order to maintain the status of the powers-that-be and the integrity of society. The woman was thus alienated from the community for 12 years. In Kinukawa's interpretation of the story, the woman as the active agent bringing about her own healing is stressed. Through overcoming the barrier set by the purity laws and touching Jesus' cloak, she triggered a miracle. As a nameless woman with low social status, she edged her way into the center of Jesus' circle, inviting the scorn of the disciples and challenging the authority of the time. Through affirming her faith and healing her, Jesus also became a 'boundary breaker', accepting her challenge to authority as valuable and legitimate. As a result of her action, she became whole, not just physically, but also socially as an accepted member of society.

Kinukawa argues that the social stigma of women, minorities and other outcasts is a result of 'labeling' by those in power. The healing of the hemorrhaging woman points to the need to break down boundaries between people, restore wholeness and challenge those exercising authority. Kinukawa challenges the Japanese churches to eradicate all forms of social prejudice, to support the rights of women, and to work for the minority Koreans, who live as second-class citizens in Japan. While one might argue whether the honor and shame system existing in the ancient Mediterranean world can be compared cross-culturally to the Japanese system, Kinukawa does illustrate how a sociological and rhetorical approach can relate the Bible to the present problems of Japan.

A Postcolonial Interpretation

In the past several years, I have tried to introduce postcolonial theory to the feminist interpretation of the Bible in Asia. There is no standard and uniformly accepted definition of 'postcolonial'. For some, *post-* refers to the period after the colonies have regained independence. For others, it also includes the period beginning with the onset of colonialism and continues into the present, when colonialism gives way to neocolonialism. Postcolonial theory has emerged in many professional fields in the work of scholars with markedly divergent interests, engaged in different critical enterprises. It has been used as a critique of Western hegemony, a subset of postmodernism and poststructuralism and a reading practice that goes against the grain.

The story of the Syrophoenician woman allows for an illustration of some of the strategies of a postcolonial reading of biblical texts (Kwok 1995b: 71-83). The Syrophoenician woman is a Canaanite woman, a Gentile whose story is recorded in the canonical gospels of Matthew (15.21-28) and Mark (7.24-30). The first important question to ask is 'How is the woman presented in the framework of the narrative?' The postcolonial theory of Indian critic Gayatri Chakravorty Spivak is particularly illuminating here. Her works expose the power dynamics underlying the manner in which colonized people are inscribed in texts and how they are consigned often to signify the Other in history (see her 1987, 1990). Citing *Jane Eyre* by Emily Brontë as an example, Spivak points out that the figure of the madwoman in the attic is signified by Bertha Mason, a white woman from Jamaica. Spivak accuses many feminist critics of overlooking the imperialist impulse that set the stage for Brontë's story (Spivak 1985: 244-47).

In the story of the Syrophoenician woman, both the woman's action and her speech point to the unequal position between her and Jesus. In Mark's account, she comes and bows down before Jesus. At the end, she is a spectator, witnessing the miracle performed by someone else. In Matthew's account, the woman is more active: is shouting when she appears before Jesus, continues to shout and then kneels before him. In both versions, her body language shows clearly that she is the one begging for a favor.

In Mark the woman does not speak for herself, rather her request is reported indirectly by the narrator (v. 26). In Matthew, she is given a voice, making her petition three times. When Jesus refuses at first to grant her request, her response—'Yes, Lord, even the dogs under the table eat the children's crumbs'—is neither confrontational nor argumentative. Interested in maintaining the relationship even when Jesus seems rude, she speaks in supportive and affirmative ways. The unequal position of the woman as portrayed in the narrative is set in a dense web of oppositions: Jewish homeland/foreign lands, inside/outside the house, Jews/Gentiles, cleanliness/uncleanliness, children/dogs, disciples/woman, and people with faith/people without faith.

Second, a postcolonial interpretation makes the connection between colonialism, sexism and anti-Judaism in this particular story. In the traditional 'salvation history' scheme of interpretation, the fact that Jesus entered a foreign land and spoke with a Gentile woman is taken to mean a beginning of the mission to the Gentiles. Salvation comes first to the house of Israel, but when Israel fails to keep the covenant with God, the Gentiles replace the Jews in inheriting God's kingdom. In the nineteenth-century heyday of colonialism, there was a concommitant trend in philology, literature and history that portrayed the Orientals in the Middle East (including the Jews) as subordinate to the Aryan race. The Semitic languages were regarded as crude and underdeveloped, while the Indo-European languages were regarded as polished, civilized and more philosophical. Christianity, superseding Judaism, was regarded as the highest form of religion. Using the Syrophoenician woman's story as their pretext, missionaries condemned all other religions as idolatrous and supersitious in order to justify their mission to the 'uncivilized' and the 'heathens'. In one broad stroke, anti-Judaism was linked with ethnocentrism and the colonial impulse.

The subordination of a female Gentile should not escape our notice in the complex gender politics of colonialism. In the history of the interpretation of the story, the woman was interpreted either as having great faith or her humility was taken as a prime example of Christian virtue. In the colonial setting, the colonizers often regarded themselves as male and the colonized, female. The humility of a female Gentile in this story could be used to reinforce a passive, docile and obedient attitude toward the dominant masters who came to conquer and rule. Just like the Syrophoenician woman, colonized peoples were expected to be subservient, as loyal as a 'devoted dog'.

Third, a postcolonial reading takes full account of the Syrophoenician woman's multiple identities. As a Gentile woman with a daughter with an unspeakable disease, she is despised by Jews and oppressed as a woman in a patriarchal society. But as a Greek-speaking woman, she also comes from the elite urban class and has the potential of being an oppressor exploiting the Galilean hinterland, which serves as the 'breadbasket' of the wealthy city of Tyre. Her multiple identities remind us to analyze marginalization in its myriad ways and caution us that there is always the Other within the Other. Furthermore, postcolonial critics challenge any simple dualistic caricature of the power dynamics behind domination/submission, insider/outsider, powerful/powerless and colonizer/colonized. A postcolonial reading insists that the woman should not be treated solely as a sexualized subject because of her gender, because her identity is also shaped by class, language, ethnicity and so on. Such a reading makes room for a consideration of the differences among women, because it does not focus solely on the sex/gender system at work in the story.

Scripture as Performance

In many parts of Asia, sacred scripture becomes part of the culture of the people because it is re-enacted in songs, drama, dance, folk arts and theater. Not only is scripture recited and chanted in holy places, it is performed during festivals and celebrations whenever the community gathers together. Art and aesthetic beauty both play an important role in Asian people's religiosity. In recent years, some pioneers have tried to use drama and theater as the medium for interpreting biblical stories. A noted example is Yuko Yuasa's use of Noh drama in Japan.

Noh drama originated in the ancient farming community of Japan as popular performance ritual depicting stories about the gods and the ancestors. Even today when Japan has become so modernized and urban, many people still enjoy Noh theater as a traditional art form. The myths, legends, folklores, poems and stories that have been preserved in oral tradition have offered Noh writers their main sources of inspiration. Noh drama employs stylized movements accompanied by songs and music to express feelings and moods. Wearing a mask that covers the entire face, the performer must express the emotion through very subtle and nuanced movements. The stage of Noh drama is simple and sparsely decorated. A screen separates the front and back stage, signifying this world and the world beyond. Many Noh dramas deal with the recurrent problems of existence, such as life and death, sickness, growing old, loss, suffering and betrayal. Most audiences that go to Noh performances know the script and follow the performance easily. The theater provides an occasion for meditation on issues of life and for collective catharsis.

Since Noh drama is a traditional performative art with many rules and regulations, it is not easy to use it to depict stories and scenes from another culture. In 1995, working with performing artists and musicians in Kyoto, Japan, Yuko Yuasa successfully staged the premiere of a biblical Noh drama entitled 'Magdalene Dancing in Crimson'. For Yuasa, the Bible and Noh drama share numerous themes. The two can be brought quite easily into dialogue with one another:

> A Biblical Noh drama is neither a biblical story told in the form of Noh, nor an interpretation of Noh stories in the light of the Bible. A Biblical Noh drama is an attempt to realize on stage the special spirituality shared by the Bible and Noh (Yuasa 1996: 2).

The life of Mary Magdalene is completely changed by her encounter with Jesus, and she follows him to the cross. Her meeting with Jesus after his resurrection is a scene well suited for the Noh stage. The drama focuses on Magdalene's subjective responses to Jesus' death and resurrection through movements, songs and pauses. It touches on the popular themes of Noh drama, including the awareness of eternity in life, love as stronger than death and insights about human nature. An exerpt from the first scene of 'Magdalene Dancing in Crimson' gives us an idea of the form of Noh drama:

> MARY: I am a woman living around here. The maple leaves scatter on the water, just like brocade. I live as a friend of the maple trees.
> MONK: Indeed a friend of the maple trees is a friend of ours. We share a certain common fate, having the same heart.
> MARY: We have met in this mountain path.
> MONK: As friends.
> MARY: Long ago, when I first met Jesus, long ago when I first met Jesus, I was a floating dancer, possessed by seven devils. I wandered aimlessly, with my sleeves soaked with tears. One day Jesus regarded me and called me, 'Mary, come to me'. Touched by the light in his eyes, I turned away completely from the floating life of old. Since that day my sleeves are never so again. Since that day completely clean and fresh, completely clean and fresh, my sleeves and myself.
> CHORUS: In this world nothing is stable.
> Bearing the sins of the world, he walked the way of sorrow to Golgotha.
> His disciples ran away, but I followed him, with his mother, to the foot of the cross.
> The sinless son of God bore the sins of the world. The sun hid in darkness.
> At dark dawn I went to the tomb to anoint the body of Jesus. Who will roll away the large stone from the tomb?
> MARY: But the large stone was rolled away.

CHORUS: and the body of Jesus was gone! How can I live if even his body is lost?
JESUS: Mary!
CHORUS: Jesus stood right behind Mary.
JESUS: Why do you seek for my love in the past? Is love not life after life? Love is forgiveness. Love is eternal. Love lives after death.
MARY AND JESUS: Love is life after life. Love is forgiveness limitless. Love is eternal. Love lives after death… (Yuasa 1996: 3)

Yuasa's 'Magdalene Dancing in Crimson' explores the theater as a form of liturgy and ministry. She emphasizes the psychological effects of Noh drama on women's spirituality in Japan, including the expression of anger, the release of pain and the self-awareness of one's emotions. Further investigation into the social and political aspects of biblical Noh drama will be needed if the medium is put into feminist use. A hermeneutics of performative arts will need to be developed, taking into consideration the use of masks, symbolic gestures, dance and movements, which would be quite different from the hermeneutics of words, both oral and written.

Chapter Five

Speaking about God

Oh dear God
Pour your spirit
That burns in the bush
That sweeps away to bring newness
Like powerful surfs of ocean
Like mighty wind
Blowing from and to all four corners
Of the world
Purify and sanctify
To make anew
To make whole

Sun Ai Lee Park (Korea)

Living in a religiously pluralistic world, when Asian feminist theologians speak of God they are influenced by the religious language and spirituality of their cultural environment. In some of these cultures, there is not even an equivalent concept of 'God', understood as the transcendent being who creates the universe. Missionaries in China, for example, debated for centuries on how to translate the term *God* into the Chinese language. God-talk by Asian feminist theologians must take into consideration the diverse religious experiences of humankind and the challenges posed by their cultural and religious contexts.

Asian feminist theologies take on many different forms: prayers, liturgies poetry and personal reflections. Most of their theological articulations are specific to the issues of their countries, such as the reunification of Korea, the burdens of poverty, the caste system, the marriage dowry in India and the continued struggles for democracy in the Philippines. But there are also emergent concerns and themes that are being addressed by women cross-culturally. Some of these include the challenge of religious pluralism, sexism and inclusive language, feminine symbols of the divine, feminist theology and the environment and violence against women. These issues are discussed both nationally and in ecumenical regional and international gatherings.

When Asian feminists talk about God, they do not begin with the abstract discussion of the doctrine of the Trinity, the debate on the existence of God, or the affirmation of God as omnipotent, unchanging and immovable. Rather, they focus on God as the source of life and the creative, sustaining power of the universe. In a continent where many people are struggling to acquire basic necessities and human dignity, God is often seen as the compassionate one, listening to the people's cries and empowering them to face life's adversities. God is the source of hope, the power overcoming despair and the vision that brings peace amidst ethnic strife, alienation, and oppression.

God-Talk in a Religiously Pluralistic Context

It is a constant challenge for Asian theologians to talk about the Christian understanding of God in a religiously pluralistic context. Raimundo Panikkar, a religious thinker who is comfortable both in the Hindu and Christian worlds, has summarized Christian self-understanding in relation to other religions as comprising five historical periods. During the first centuries, when Christians were constantly being persecuted by the Roman state, the prevalent Christian self-consciousness might be characterized as *witnessing*. During the next period, which extends through the Middle Ages, *conversion* was the dominant mode, as people converted to Christ, responded to the monastic call and lived the Christian style of life. Then came the period of the *crusades*, when religious intolerance and economic interests resulted in centuries of warfare. The dominant feature of the next period is *mission*, when missionaries were sent to save souls and warships were commissioned to colonize peoples. It was only after the colonial empires had declined in power and the colonized peoples began to re-embrace their own cultures, that *dialogue* became a catchword (Panikkar 1987: 93-95).

It is significant to note that except for that of the first centuries, the dominant self-understanding of Christians has centered in conversion, crusade and mission. From a cross-cultural perspective, this is quite different from the self-understanding found in Confucianism, Buddhism, Daoism and other Asian religions. Process theologian Majorie Hewitt Suchocki has suggested a connection between religious imperialism and sexism in Christianity. Just as the masculine experience is universalized to define what is fully human in Christian thought, one particular religion is absolutized as normative. Religious imperialism like sexism, Suchocki argues, operates according to a superiority–inferiority syndrome, when the value and dignity of the Other is not respected (Suchoki 1987: 150-54).

In their encounter with people of other faith traditions, Asian feminist theologians have cautioned against a triumphant attitude that assumes Christianity to be superior to others. Living closely with their religious neighbors, they know that they have much to learn from the diverse experiences of the ultimate mystery and the manifold articulations of the divine in other faith traditions. Instead of being driven by a 'crusading' mind, Dulcie Abraham describes her experience as a journey with others:

> The discovery of women's spirituality and experience of God is a journey which women of all faiths are traveling both within their own religious traditions, and together with women of other faiths. It is also a journey in which both women and men together are discovering afresh their experience of God's nature and being (Abraham 1989: 4).

With humility and open-mindedness, many Asian feminist theologians recognize that God's revelation is found not only in the Bible and the Christian tradition but also in other peoples' religious experiences recorded in their sacred scriptures, myths, stories, legends and symbols. The resources for constructing theology from a multireligious context are rich and profound, if one stretches one's imagination. As Thai feminist theologian Nantawan Boonprasat Lewis has said:

> The use of one's cultural and religious tradition indicates the respect and pride of one's heritage which is the root of one's being to be authentic enough to draw as a source for theologizing. On the other hand, it demonstrates a determination of hope for possibilities beyond one's faith tradition, possibilities which can overcome barriers of human expression, including language, vision, and imagination (Lewis 1986: 21).

In a religiously pluralistic world, the ultimate, the mystery, or the sacred is known by many names. Many Asian feminist theologians believe that these different names in separate religious systems refer to realities that are totally different from that conveyed by monotheistic notions of God (Yahweh, Elohim, Allah). According to their view, while we can learn from others through religious dialogue, the Ultimate worshipped or venerated by the believers is not the same. But there is also a radical perspective arguing that the divine is a mystery, not to be pigeonholed or limited by our languages and expressions, nor boxed by our religious systems. In recent years, Chung Hyun Kyung has variously called it the 'life force', the *ki*, or the energy of raw life. She says: 'What matters to Asian women is survival and the liberation of themselves and their communities. What matters for them is not Jesus, Sakyamumi, Mohammed, Confucius, Kwan In, or Ina, but rather the life force which empowers them to claim their humanity' (Chung 1990: 113). She notices that this energy of raw life has been known by many names, many of them female: Ki, Chi, *Shakti, prana, ruah,* and in the *Dao de jing*, 'the mysterious female' or the spirit of the valley which never dries up (Chung 1996b: 139).

The attempt to go beyond the limits of human languages and symbols in naming God likewise challenges us to rethink fundamental religious concepts, such as monotheism and polytheism. In the nineteenth-century evolutionary understanding of religion, Christianity was elevated above other religions partly because it involved the worship of one God only. As Carol P. Christ has observed, monotheism usually arises in opposition to other views of divine reality, especially to those that embrace female imagery and power (Christ 1997: 112). In religiously pluralistic Asian societies, the issue of whether there is one God or many gods seems unimportant and has not created such controversy as in the West. Some Asian religious traditions, such as Buddhism and Confucianism, do not have the equivalent notion of 'God' as in Christianity. Most Asian societies have numerous male and female religious images, and feel no need to argue that a single god or goddess is superior to all others. The concept of God as a being has been influenced by a philosophy of substance, not found in many Asian philosophies. If God is not thought to exist as a countable 'being', the argument of one god or many gods does not apply. Furthermore, according to the Buddhist principle of non-duality, the one and the many are not mutually exclusive. What seem to be opposite views can be two perspectives on the same reality.

In Asian religious traditions, what one practices in life is more important than what one believes. Religion is embodied in all spheres in life, rather than in some propositions, or precepts, of beliefs. This more inclusive approach to the religiosity of humankind influences the style of theology done by Asian feminist theologians, because for them theology has much to do with spirituality. The purpose of theology is not to *define* God, but rather to express a sense of wonder, awe and grace in the presence of the living power and energy of the divine. It can be done with dance, song, ritual, poetry and movement, and not just words. As Chung Hyun Kyung has said:

> For Asian women, theology is a language of hope, dreams, and poetry. It is firmly based on concrete, historical reality but points to the mystery and vision that calls Asian women from the future and the depth of all that is… It enables them to keep moving, flowing with the rhythm of the universe even when the heartbeat of the universe seems to be destroyed by human greed and hatred… Theology as vision quest is not an escapist, otherworldly addiction of the oppressed. It is remembering the original wholeness of creation and activating the dangerous memory of the future (Chung 1990: 101).

Sexism and Inclusive Language

During the past several decades, feminist theologians in the West have persistently argued against sexism in religious language. They have pointed out that language constitutes reality, influences our thinking and consciousness, and shapes our images, behavior, attitudes and relationships. For example, if the pronoun for God is male as in the English language, people will be conditioned to think that God is indeed male. Liturgical formulas, such as 'in the name of the Father, Son, and Holy Spirit', reinforce an androcentric notion of the divine and leave out the experiences of women. Moreover, many of the metaphors and images for God in the Bible and the Christian tradition, such as king, lord, father and bridegroom are masculine. Struggling to reform the church, Western feminist theologians have drafted and created inclusive liturgies, participated in the translation of an inclusive lectionary and written hymns that include masculine and feminine metaphors for God.

The issue of inclusive language, however, has not received so much attention in the Asian churches as in the West. There are several reasons for this. First, many Asian theologians, including feminists, think that other issues, such as neocolonialism, militarism and sex-tourism, have primacy and priority over the change of religious language. They are suspicious that Western women's focus on inclusive language reflects middle-class interests and allows them to avoid confronting their exploitation of the majority of the women in the world. Second, the structures of Asian languages are quite different from that of Indo-European languages. In some cases, the term used for God does not have a gender reference and the pronoun for God is not masculine. Third, in the religiously pluralistic contexts in Asia, there are both male and female images of the divine, quite unlike the androcentric images of

God in Christian monotheism. Whereas God as Mother or as *She* may sound iconoclastic and shocking to Western ears, it does not disturb Asians to such a degree.

Let us use the Chinese language as an illustration. In classical Chinese, personal pronouns are not gender specific and refer to both male and female. When the modern Chinese language developed in the 1920s, separate pronouns for he and she were created. At the same time, a totally different pronoun for *God* was created, one that is not gender specific. Likewise, the Chinese generic term for human beings—*ren*—is an inclusive term, neither male nor female. Whereas the NRSV of the Bible has to change 'Let us create man in our image' to the inclusive 'Let us create *humankind* in our image', there is no such need for the Chinese Bible, because the inclusive term *ren* has been used consistently. Also, in the Chinese cultural and religious sensibility, there is an emphasis on the balance of heaven and earth, yang and yin, sun and moon, and the masculine and the feminine (see the discussion in Ng 1997: 21-36).

But this is not to imply that sexism does not exist in Asian languages, or that inclusive language for God is a non-issue. The androcentric nature of Chinese language can be found in the etiology of some of the Chinese characters. For example, the characters for *slave, cunning* and *adulterous* are all based on the radical for *female*, showing sexist and classist biases against women. Furthermore, it is clear that God has been imaged as a male in the terms used to translate the word *God* into the Chinese language. There are three different terms that missionaries have used to translate the term *God*, all of which are still used in the Chinese churches. Mainline Protestant churches use *shangdi*, a term from the Chinese classics, that literally means the king above. Roman Catholic missionaries combined the character for *heaven* with the character for *lord* to create a new term *tianzhu*, meaning the lord of heaven. Only the third term *shen*, referring generally to god or spirit, is gender inclusive. The Korean translation for the term *God* is *Hananim*, which is a combination of two words meaning heaven and respectful being. *Hananim* is gender inclusive, but Korean churches frequently add the word *Abuji* meaning 'father' after it, making God a male figure.

Although there has not been a strong movement in the Asian churches for the use of inclusive language, some Asian feminist theologians have spoken against the exclusion of women's experiences in theological and liturgical language. Theologian Ahn Sang Nim of Korea has condemned the exclusive imagery of God as male:

God has been perceived as a powerful male, a father with absolute power. Such a theology confessing such a patriarchal God has established a patriarchal hierarchy in a patriarchal church. In such a church, women have lost their position of equality with men and have become devalued, marginalized (Ahn 1989: 128).

In addition, Stella Faria of India insists that a change in religious language must also be accompanied by a change in attitude. For her, the language of the Bible, the lectionary and the liturgy must be scrutinized if the Eucharist is to become truly a sign and sacrament of unity. She says: 'To proclaim Christ, language must be bias free' (Faria 1988: 55). Encouraged by the Ecumenical Decade of the Churches in Solidarity of Women (1988–98), some Asian Christian women called upon the churches to examine their language in prayers, hymns, liturgy and Bible translations. For example, a group of Pakistani women meeting at Multan has named sexist language as one of the stones the churches need to roll away: 'At the baptism ceremony, the child is defined as the son or daughter of the father only… In our liturgies, we confess our sins to our brothers but often with no mention of sisters. The symbols emphasize the maleness of God, ignoring the female aspects' (Azariah *et al.* 1989: 49).

Most of the hymns sung in the Asian churches are translations of Western hymns and many contain male images of God. But the inclusive language movement has made inroads into ecumenical circles. Some of the new hymns in the hymnody published by the Christian Conference of Asia, *Sounding the Bamboo*, use inclusive language. Gatherings of Asian women and theologians have created and experimented with forms of worship and liturgies that use indigenous symbols and inclusive language. For example, the following meditation was used in the workshop on Women in the New Creation in Hong Kong in 1997:

In the beginning God made the World!
Made it and mothered it,
Shaped it and fathered it;
Filled it with seed and with signs of fertility.
Filled it with love and with ability.
All that is green, blue, deep and growing,
God's is the hand that created you.
All that crawls, flies, swims, walks or is motionless,
God's is the hand that created you.
All that suffers, lacks, despairs
God's is the hand that created you (AWRC: 12).

Feminine Images of God

Some Western feminists argue that the male images of God in Christianity have contributed to the denigration of women's body and sexuality. Meanwhile, there has been a rebirth of interest in goddesses and a revival of goddess-oriented spirituality in both Europe and North America during the past two decades. Women have established home altars, formed small ritual circles, and composed songs, dances and prayers to honor the Goddess, overturning what has been suppressed in Western culture and religion. Carol P. Christ has argued that the images of the Goddess affirm women's body as powerful, strong and sensual, connecting women to nature's power of transformation and regeneration (Christ 1997). While some Western feminists have embarked only recently on a search for the goddesses of prehistoric Europe, Asian women have always been surrounded by strong female religious figures.

The issue of feminine representations of the divine has been a focus of Asian feminist theologians since the late 1980s. In the two interfaith dialogues among Asian women held in 1989 and 1991 by the Asian Women's Centre for Culture and Theology, female images of God in Asian religious traditions was the subject of discussion. Some Asian feminist theologians were looking for ways to overcome the one-sided androcentric portrayal of the divine in Asian churches, and they wanted to learn something from their indigenous traditions. They have researched the development of goddesses in different historical epochs and the relationships of women to these goddesses.

The worship of goddesses and the feminine images of the divine have a very long history in Asia, dating back to prehistoric times. In China, neolithic sites for offering gifts to the Earth Mother have been excavated and female figurines symbolizing goddesses have been discovered. In Japan, the sun goddess is the ancestor of the Japanese emperor; in Tibet, the goddess Tara is considered grandmother of the people as a whole. Before the Spanish colonization, Filipino legends and creation stories referred to Ina as their earth mother. Female images of the divine abound in Korean shamanism. In China today, one of the most important female religious figures is Guanyin (the Buddhist Bodhisattva of Mercy), although this Bodhisattva is male in India and Tibet. India has a rich and living tradition of goddesses and female epic heroines dating back to medieval times. Sita, Durga, Kali and Sarasvati are mothers, consorts, daughters, sisters and even protectors of the male deities and heroes. These goddesses are worshiped by both women and men in Asia, and unlike in the Mesopotamian and prehistoric Europe, they have not been superseded by the male gods of patriarchal religion.

The goddesses in the Asian religious traditions play many different roles, which are not limited to the stereotypical functions of mothering and nurturing. In a study of Korean goddesses, Choi Man Ja has listed that the goddesses have exhibited the following diverse roles: controlling nature, sustaining life, founding the Korean nation and protecting the villages. Goddesses appear also as spirits of the house and of ancestors, or as resentful spirits who demand justice and resolution. Korean goddesses have been portrayed as independent and powerful, preserving life and sustaining survival, having profound wisdom, acting as saviors, demanding justice and furnishing hope (Choi 1991: 180-90). In the Indian context, as Stella Faria points out, goddesses symbolize not only motherhood, beauty and fertility but also wisdom, learning, intellect, eloquence, power, charity and creativity. Some of the goddesses act in concert with their male counterparts, as in the case of Parvati and Siva. Nevertheless, their relationship can be characterized as one of partnership and equality (Faria 1989: 7-17). In China, Nüwa was credited for having created the entire universe, and the powerful goddess Mazu, worshiped in the coastal areas of China and Taiwan, is the patron deity of sea-farers and fishing folks.

But the existence of strong traditions of goddesses in Asia does not imply that the status of women in society is any higher. Very often, the power of the goddesses was controlled or tamed in order to serve patriarchal purposes, and attempts have been made to modify traditions surrounding female deities. For example, in Korea, the female mythological figures who were founders of nations were transformed to be consorts of male figures as the legends evolved. Guanyin is worshiped for her compassion and power in bestowing sons on women, instead of being remembered as a strong woman who rebels against her father's will. In India, women are taught to emulate the chastity, endurance and wifely devotion of Sita, who chose to immolate herself in a show of fidelity and loyalty, and to protect her husband's honor.

When Asian feminist theologians want to recover female images and metaphors for God, they should pay attention to the lessons gleaned from history. First, female representation of the divine meets a deeply felt religious need of all Asian people, both men and women. Even the missionaries recognized this and tried to use the devotion to the Virgin

Mary in Roman Catholicism to galvanize support for their evangelistic efforts. At the same time, some of the devotions to Mary, Fatima and other female saints can be used to reinforce submission, obedience and docility in women. Second, the female symbols should not be limited to the mothering and nurturing roles of women alone, but extend to other dimensions, such as strength, wisdom, power and creativity. Third, Asian feminist theologians must encourage and devise strategies to introduce inclusive language and symbols into the liturgy and life of local churches. Otherwise, such innovative ideas will not take root in the communities of faith.

Asian feminist theologians have sought to reinterpret the figure of Mary, the mother of Jesus. Instead of presenting Mary as a gentle, docile and sanctified mother, some Asian feminist theologians have reclaimed her as a model of the fully liberated human being. As a virgin, she is a self-defining woman, not subject to other human beings; as a mother, she is the giver of life; and as a sister, she stands in solidarity with other oppressed women. Mary is also recognized as a model of true discipleship. She accepts the challenge of God, lives in faith and helps to found the earliest community of faith. Mary is the co-redeemer in human salvation. In the Philippines, Mapa, the dark-skinned Madonna, is believed to be the mother of the poor and protector of the people in their struggle against colonialism (Chung 1990: 74-84). Just as Latin American feminist theologians have rediscovered the liberating potential of the figure of Mary, so too, some Asian Christian women, especially those in the Roman Catholic tradition, have reclaimed her as a patron of their persistent fight for dignity and equality.

God as Creative Power of Life

Most Asian religious traditions are deeply cosmological, and there is no dualistic separation of the divine and the human, or the divine and the natural world. In India, for example, shakti is the power, the feminine energy, or the energizing force of all divinity, all humanity and all creation. In China, the Dao is the principle, or the all-embracing force, that undergirds and transforms all things in the universe. In Korean shamanism, the spiritual realm can be brought to interact with the human realm through dance, drums, bells and rituals. Living in such an environment in which poetry, landscape paintings and aesthetics constantly evoke the sacredness of nature, Asian feminist theologians have an intimate sense that God is immanent in nature, sustaining and replenishing creation.

The tendency to see each part in connection with the whole in Asian philosophical tradition is very different from the atomistic, mechanistic and individualistic worldview found in the West, influenced by the development of modern science and Enlightenment philosophy. This sense of the interrelatedness of all things and the humility before the awesome cosmos is illustrated by this famous passage by a Chinese philosopher:

> Heaven is my father and earth is my mother, and even such a small being as I finds an intimate place in their minds. Therefore, that which fills the universe I regard as my body and that which directs the universe I regard as my nature. All people are my brothers and sisters, and all things are my companions (Chan 1969: 496).

Heaven, earth, mountains, trees, rain, rivers and seeds are recurrent motifs in East Asian poetry and painting. They are also found abundantly in the Bible. For example, Second Isaiah declares that the day when the Israelites embark on a new exodus, the mountains and the hills shall burst into song and the trees in the fields shall clap their hands (Isa. 55.12). These images are not mere metaphorical devices or literary embellishments, because they serve to bring out an important dimension of the prophet's understanding of God: that God acts both in nature and history, that historical events have a lot to do with the cosmological realm, and vice versa.

Many Asian feminist theologians have begun to move away from a hierarchical, dualistic and patriarchal notion of God to a model that is ecological, feminist and organic. The hierarchal model stresses the transcendence of God, that God is the 'wholly other', infinitely above human beings and all creation. A dualistic understanding posits a binary opposition between nature and humans, male and female, God and the world. A patriarchal and anthropocentric model imagines God as king, father, and lord. A feminist and ecological approach points to God as non-intrusive, inclusive and sustaining, and it uses inclusive images and female metaphors to describe God, including non-anthropomorphic ones. An organic worldview respects the interdependence, diversity and inherent value of all life forms.

Cosmological awareness leads many Asian feminist theologians to accent God's immanence over God's transcendence. The immanence of God is found both within us and in all God's creation. The idea of panentheism (all-in-God) has close affinity with Asian religiosity. We can come to know God through nature as well as through human history. There is no separation between 'special revelation', known through the specific Christian story and the so-called 'general revelation', known through nature and wisdom from other cultures. Marlene Perera, a Catholic sister from Sri Lanka, has come to a deeper appreciation of God's immanence through religious dialogue with her Buddhist friends:

> More and more we must acquire the eastern approach to God. That is that God is a very deep, authentic, liberating and life-giving experience rather than the unreachable other up above. God is not up above but deep down. God is within: within me, within humanity, its aspirations, struggles, strivings and history and we need to touch this life-giving Spirit to find liberation (Perera 1991: 209).

God, immanent in the entire universe, affirms life over against forces of death. This eco-centered or life-centered emphasis is emerging clearly in the eco-feminist writings from Asia. Aruna Gnanadason, for example, denounces the dualisms of mind/body, spirit/flesh, culture/nature, men/women which influenced Western patriarchal theology and have in turn been absorbed by inherited Third World theology. Her understanding of God is shaped by Indian cosmology, which affirms the interdependence of all forms of life, the dialectical harmony between human beings and nature, as well as between male and female principles. This holistic vision becomes a source from which eco-feminist theology draws its inspiration in India (Gnanadason 1996: 74-81).

God as the creative power of life constantly sustains and renews creation. This ecological understanding of God calls for a *recycling* of Christian tradition so that the usable past can be brought to illumine the present, and what is useless be left behind. That God is not separated from creation means that the destruction of the environment because of human greed is an assault against the fullness of God. Human beings are part of nature and their salvation is closely linked to the diversity, balance and well-being of the earth. God, the source of power to call forth a 'new heaven and new earth', is the symbol of our hope in our present ecological crisis.

The Compassionate God

Many Asian feminists point to the compassionate nature of God in their theological reflections. Katoppo titled her book *Compassionate and Free*, and the first anthology by Third World women was called *With Passion and Compassion.* Buddhism captures the religious imagination of so many Asian people, and increasingly people in the West too, partly because of its teaching about compassion for human suffering, for all sentient beings and for the earth. As the Dalai Lama has said:

> We should have this [compassion] from the depths of our heart, as if it were nailed there. Such compassion is not merely concerned with a few sentient beings such as friends and relatives, but extends up to the limits of the cosmos, in all directions and towards all beings throughout space (1979: 111).

In Confucianism, what distinguishes a human being from other animals is not her reasoning faculty or intellect but her ability to show *ren* toward others. *Ren* is a difficult word to translate, often rendered as 'benevolence', 'love' or even 'humanity'. All these attributes are integral parts of the Chinese understanding of the term *compassion.*

Since the concept of compassion has such profound connotations in Asian traditions, the understanding of God as compassionate is multifaceted and pluralistic in Asian theological discourse. Not only female theologians, but male theologians speak about the compassionate character of God. As C.S. Song has said, 'God moves on in compassion. We have no alternative but to move on with God toward that vision of a community of compassion and communion of love' (1982: 260). In Asian feminist discourse, there are three themes that are closely related to the compassion of God: justice, community and wisdom.

Compassion is not sentimental love. It is a profound reverence toward life, empathy toward those who suffer, and concern for the flourishing of all beings. The compassionate God listens to the cries and supplications of the Asian people, as God listened to the slaves in bondage during Moses' time. Asian feminist theologians usually begin their reflections by analyzing the oppression and suffering of the Asian people. They do not want to give the impression that all Asians, and women in particular, are victims. But they wish to express their care and solidarity with all those who suffer, because they believe God cares and listens. As Lee Oo Chung writes: 'God stands on the side of the downtrodden. Being always on the side of oppressed and suffering women, God experiences their pain with them, giving them the courage and wisdom to overcome, and helping them arrive at the final victory' (Lee 1994: 120).

The compassion of God, however, is more than divine retribution or a demand for righteousness. Traditional Asian philosophies seldom speak of justice in the Aristotelian sense of giving each one what is due to him or her. Justice is grounded not so much in the language of 'equality' or 'rights' in Asian religiosity, but in compassion for all living things. To affirm that God is compassionate is to acknowledge that the ultimate source of life is good and that the moral nature of the universe is characterized by mutuality, caring and interdependence, and not by ruthless exploitation and greed.

The compassionate God creates the universe and establishes relationship with all creatures. In the Genesis story, God creates Adam and Eve so that human beings do not live alone, but in communion with God, with fellow human beings and with the earth community. Most Asian cultures emphasize the radical relationality of human existence. A person does not exist in isolation, but in the web of relationships in which she finds herself. While Western post-industrialized societies often understand human beings in an atomic, individualistic way, Asian cultures see a person-in-relation. Human beings cannot live in peace, in shalom, with one another without first establishing a relationship that is reciprocal and respectful. Different human groups will continue to engage in genocide, war and other atrocities without aiming at a higher ideal to build communities of compassion and solidarity. Asian Christian women believe their motivation and inspiration lies in a God who is compassionate and relational.

Compassion is not associated with the stereotypical feminine virtues of gentility, kind-heartedness and mercy in Asian traditions. In Tibetan Buddhism, for example, compassion is symbolized by the male and wisdom by the female. The union of wisdom and compassion is a manifestation of enlightenment in Buddhist spirituality. In the Christian tradition, *agape* and *sophia* (wisdom) are also important manifestations of the divine. Agape is God's unconditional love and the female symbol of Sophia has played an increasing role in feminist spirituality. In the Asian context, Rosario Battung, a Catholic sister and a Zen teacher from the Philippines characterizes wisdom and compassion as the way for integration and cosmic interwoveness. The highest spiritual ideal, for her, is becoming one's true self in community with all beings in a harmonious and well-ordered universe. She finds the metaphor 'God the Mother' as conveying most adequately the wisdom and compassion of the divine. God the Mother is the giver of breath, who brings forth life, continually sustains and nurtures us, challenging us to bring forth her reign of wisdom and love (Battung 1993: 46-47).

Chapter Six

Christology

Our christologies are not only interpretations of Jesus, but confessions of our faith in this Jesus who has made a difference in our lives, and not only as a speculative activity, but as active engagement in striving towards the full humanity Jesus came to bring.

Virginia Fabella (Philippines)

'Who do you say that I am?' Each generation must answer this question in their own time. For Christian women in Asia, this question brings into sharp focus the issues of Christian identity, gospel and culture, sin and redemption and the nature of the Christian movement. Asian feminist theologians must assess critically the images of Christ promulgated by missionaries during the colonial era. For example, the myth of the uniqueness of Jesus Christ fuels Christian triumphalism and exclusivity. Living closely among non-Christians in most Asian countries, Asian feminist theologians reformulate their christological understanding taking into consideration interactions with people of other faiths. A critical dialogue is sought between the Christian understanding of Christ and other soteriological motifs found within their cultures and histories.

Since most Asian countries were colonies of Western powers, the influences of colonization on Christology must be subject to close scrutiny. During the colonial period, the Christ figure was invariably interpreted through a Western lens and forced upon the colonized peoples without paying any attention to their social predicament or seeking to enter into a dialogue with their indigenous traditions. The debate on whether Jesus was fully human or divine has little meaning in some cultural and linguistic contexts. The message of salvation, if concerned primarily with redeeming individual souls and life after death, has little relevance in an Asia plagued by issues of survival under foreign domination. Even today, Christianity is still seen as a foreign religion by the majority of Asians, largely because of this 'Western captivity' of Christianity.

Moreover, the images of Christ proclaimed during colonial times justified the domination of the oppressors. For example, the suffering and death of Jesus was glorified and his silent endurance held up as a model to be followed. Jesus as the suffering servant was used to inculcate submission and obedience among the subjugated. Another image was that of Jesus as Lord, which had political as well as religious overtones. The belief that Jesus is the Lord of the universe justified the domination of other peoples and their lands for Christ's sake. The lordship of a male Christ not only undergirded colonialism, but lent its support to patriarchal dominance in the church and society as well. As Korean theologian Kim Yong Bock has noted, Christ came as the conqueror and crusader of the 'pagans' and 'heathens' during Western expansion, and later as 'promoter of Western capitalism', and as 'transmitter of Western civilization'. Such a Christ has very little to do with the suffering and struggling peoples of Asia (Kim 1990: 14).

In their quest for a new understanding of Christology, Asian feminist theologians have challenged the language, models and frameworks used by Western theologians, especially by the male elites. They have reclaimed their cultural roots and experimented with different images and metaphors for Christ, using idioms and language from their own contexts. They exhibit creativity and freedom in their theological imagination, not limited by the parameters set by Western debates. At the same time, they are not blind to the patriarchal elements in their indigenous cultures, and look especially toward women's popular religion as resources. They attempt to lift up women's vision of hope and aspiration for themselves, their communities and the planet earth.

Asian feminist theologians find that they have to reinterpret sin and redemption anew in the contemporary context. The traditional emphasis on the individual and spiritual dimension of sin proves to be less than helpful for women. Women are not just sinners; they are the *sinned against* too. Many Asian women suffer as outcasts of their society, not because of any innate human depravity or moral deficiency, but because of the social and institutional violence that dehumanizes and marginalizes them. A new understanding of sin must reflect the socio-political and the religio-cultural realities. Furthermore, as Valerie Saiving and other feminist theologians have pointed out, defining sin as pride, egotism and sexual aggression betrays an androcentric bias, because such characteristics are more likely to be displayed by men in a patriarchal society. The sins of women are more likely to be passivity, the lack of a strong ego, acquiescence, sloth and accepting fate as their lot (Goldstein: 1960: 100-12).

Redemption comprises, therefore, not only personal and spiritual reconciliation with God, but also liberation from bondage, the opportunity to develop one's potential, the well-being of one's family and community, the freedom from warfare and other forms of violence, the availability of a life-sustaining eco-system and a sense of hope and security for the future. As we have seen in previous chapters, Lee Oo Chung uses the biblical term *shalom* to describe this state of well-being, while Mananzan has called it *total liberation*, in which women's liberation is an integral part. Gnanadason uses the ecological language of respect for life and a wholistic vision of interdependence to articulate her hope.

How do the death and resurrection of Christ fit into this historical and ecological drama of redemption? Are the different theories of atonement in Western Christianity relevant here? One controversial issue is how to interpret the suffering of Jesus on the cross. African-American theologian Delores Williams suggests that the image of the body of Jesus dripping blood is not helpful for black women because it glorifies unjust suffering. Jesus as the surrogate victim who suffers for humanity evokes painful memories of black women who were often coerced into surrogate roles during slavery and even after emancipation. The cross, used to justify slavery and genocide, must be confronted as a symbol of evil, and what is redemptive is not Jesus' death, but his life and prophetic ministry (Williams 1991: 1-14).

Still, from within the complex context of Asia, the suffering of Jesus must be seen in a nuanced and multilayered way. Asian feminist theologians do not condone innocent suffering and sacrifice. They are against all forms of religious ideology—whether within Christianity or their indigenous traditions—that inflicts senseless suffering because of social injustice. On the other hand, they recognize that the language of suffering is powerful and profound in the traditions of Asia, and it must be interpreted with reference to their various cultural milieu. In cultures shaped by Buddhism, for example, suffering is seen as inevitable in human existence. The fact that Jesus suffers shows that he is fully human, a co-sufferer with humanity. Jesus does not belong to the oppressors; he is one of the *minjung* (the masses). Many Christian women in Asia identify with such a compassionate God who suffers in solidarity with them, listens to their cries and responds to their pleas.

But just as the Buddhist acknowledgment of suffering as inevitable has the danger, when misunderstood, of encouraging passive submission to one's fate, the Christian glorification of Jesus' innocent suffering has the danger of condoning victimization, of finding scapegoats and of accepting sacrifice as salvific. The task for Asian feminist theologians is to find ways to speak of suffering that respect Asian women's religiosity, while pointing out that suffering is not their lot, because suffering can be transformed. Jesus' resurrection transforms death and suffering, and Jesus' life and ministry bear witness to his commitment to justice and the welfare of the marginalized.

Approaches to Christology

Since the religious, cultural and political contexts of the Asian feminist theologians are so diverse, their approaches to Christology vary widely. To illustrate the richness of the feminist theological imagination and to highlight the influences of context on reconstruction of Christology, I shall discuss four representative approaches from the Filipino, Korean, Chinese and Indian contexts. Nevertheless, these four approaches do not exhaust the many possibilities for feminist reflections on Christ in Asia; for within each cultural context, a plurality of voices arise. The following examples have been selected to demonstrate some innovative attempts at dialogue between Christian faith and Asian indigenous traditions and social contexts.

Jesus as a Fully Liberated Human Being

The Philippine islands were colonized by Spain for more than 300 years and by the United States for about 50 years. Since independence, the Filipino people have struggled both against neocolonialism and against the lengthy dictatorial rule of the Marco regime. Filipino feminist theology emerged out of involvement in political movements during the 1970s, especially in the people's power movement, which brought Cory Aquino to power in 1986. With a Christian population of 92 percent, the Philippines shares commonalities politically and culturally with Latin American countries more than with other Asian nations. Not surprisingly, Latin American liberation theology, developing out of the long struggles against colonialism and the misguided development programs dictated by American capitalism, captures the theological imagination of progressive Filipino theologians. Several leading Filipino feminist theologians speak of Jesus as the liberator, or Jesus as a fully liberated human.

Mary John Mananzan has outlined the emerging methodology developed by EATWOT Women's Commission, which is helpful to understand feminist theology in the Philippines. The starting point is contextualization, which highlights the experience of Asian women and their struggle in a patriarchal world. Women must then engage in religious and cultural critique, exposing the elements that perpetuate women's subordination. This is followed by the recovery of the authentic value of women's experience, especially their religious heritage, while rejecting imposed traditions. As women bring their traditions to bear on the critical issues they face, a reinterpretation and reformulation is necessary to find new language, symbols and religious forms with which to respond to the historical moment. The last step is envisioning new possibilities for the community and devising action to fulfill these possibilities (Mananzan 1992: 93).

Filipino feminist theologians began their christological search by analyzing women's situations and the ways women are influenced by popular religiosity. Mananzan notes that Spanish religiosity and its Mexican adaptation decisively influence the images of Christ in the Philippines. The traditional Spanish Christ is rather docetic with little connection to real life, a Christ that leaps from the infant Christ to the Christ on the cross. During the period of Spanish colonization, the image of the suffering Christ was highlighted, with an annual procession during Holy Week, the reading of the Passion narrative and the re-enactment of the suffering and death of Christ. The festivities were meant to inculcate loyalty to Spain and to the Church, and to preach a passive acceptance of events in this world, looking for reward and salvation in the afterlife. While Good Friday was dramatized, there was no concomitant celebration of Easter, the beginning of new life (Mananzan 1993: 87-88). By emphasizing the mortal suffering of a beaten, scourged and defeated Christ as well as a spiritualized salvation in the other world, the Christian message was used to legitimize the colonial order by pacifying the people.

Reinterpreting Jesus' suffering is crucial for Filipino feminist theology since many Filipino women have internalized the fact that the crucified Jesus understands their suffering, which they passively and resignedly endure (Fabella and Park 1989: 10). One strategy is to reclaim the subversive aspects of the Passion story in the people's revolutionary movements. Mananzan observes that even when the Spanish colonizers used the Passion narrative as a tool of oppression, Filipino people drew from it much of the language of anti-colonialism in the late nineteenth century. The suffering, death and resurrection of Jesus, and the day of judgment inspired the millennial beliefs that enabled the peasantry to take action for their liberation. Suffering is neither the end nor salvific by itself, for there is judgment and resurrection as promised by God (Mananzan 1993: 87-88). Another strategy is to distinguish between the 'passive' and 'active' moments of Jesus' suffering. Lydia Lascano, a community organizer, identifies women's oppression under colonialism, militarism and patriarchy with Jesus' passive suffering. But what is more important is Jesus' active suffering, which is his presence in Filipino women's struggle for justice, accompanying and identifying with them in their march to freedom (Lascano 1985: 121-29). The image of the suffering servant, therefore, should not be used to justify the victimization of women and to condone unjust suffering.

Filipino feminist theologians' images of Christ are not static, but change over time, as their political and feminist consciousness deepens. For example, Mananzan notes that her own image of Christ has changed from the gentle Jesus in her novitiate days, to the angry Christ when she first participated in worker's struggles, and to Jesus as the fully liberated and liberating human being when she became more deeply involved in social struggles (Mananzan 1988: 12-13). Virginia Fabella, too, is inspired by the liberating Christ:

> In the light of Asian women's reality in general, a liberational, hope-filled, love-inspired, and praxis-oriented christology is what holds meaning for me. In the person and praxis of Jesus are found the grounds of our liberation from all oppression and discrimination: whether political or economic, religious or cultural, or based on gender, race or ethnicity. Therefore the image of Jesus as liberator is consistent with my christology (Fabella and Park 1989: 10).

There are several dimensions to Filipino feminist theologians' understanding of Jesus as a fully liberated human being. First, the accent is on Jesus' life and ministry, and not so much on his death and passion. During his life time, Jesus befriended the underdogs of society and challenged both the Jewish religious authorities and the Roman leadership. He displayed a remarkably considerate attitude toward women and treated them with respect. Several times in his life, he transgressed religious and ethnic boundaries, extending his ministry to people such as

the Samaritan woman and the Syrophoenician woman. Second, Jesus'
central message is the kingdom of God, a reign of peace and justice that
is meant for everyone. Women as well as men have a place in God's
reign. To enter the kingdom, one must repent and change one's way of
living and behaving (Fabella and Park 1989: 5-6). Third, Jesus was
imbued with an inner freedom that liberated him from the yoke of
material things, from an oppressive bondage to the Law, and from the
undue influence of respect for human authorities (Mananzan 1988: 13).
Fourth, Jesus' passion m⟨...⟩   ⟨...⟩ith the promise of
⟨...⟩   ⟨...⟩mission fails, for his
⟨...⟩' death reveals the
⟨...⟩nkind and Jesus'
⟨...⟩he experience of
⟨...⟩ist, which is itself
⟨...⟩ple to have the
⟨...⟩rity (Mananzan

⟨...⟩ogians are not
⟨...⟩ a male figure.
⟨...⟩ned whether a
⟨...⟩Asian feminist
⟨...⟩nted out, the
⟨...⟩ ontological
⟨...⟩ 1988: 113).
⟨...⟩ves that Jesus
⟨...⟩vomen with

⟨...⟩ J⟨...⟩
h⟨...⟩
di⟨...⟩   ⟨...⟩ore effectively the male
de⟨...⟩   ⟨...⟩and show the way to a right and just male-female
relationship, challenging both men and women to change their life
pattern' (unpublished paper quoted in Mananzan 1988: 14).

While the image of Christ as a fully liberated human being may hold
promise in the predominantly Christian context of the Philippines,
other cultures hold other role models or patterns for a truly humanized
person, such as Confucius or Gandhi. It may be helpful in the future to
compare these various patterns and to lift up female role models as well.
Furthermore, Latin American liberation theology has undergone a process of self-scrutiny in the light of the transformation of the former
Soviet Union and Eastern Europe. The commitment to the poor is reaf-
firmed, but the promise of the socialist analysis and the strategies for

[handwritten margin notes:]
Filipino
• Spanish colonizers used passion as tool of oppression
• male-female
• make greater use of pre-colonial religiosity to find new symbols 86.

liberation need to be updated under current circumstances. Filipino theology in general, and Filipino feminist theology in particular, need to re-examine their own frameworks of analysis. Future christological attempts need to make greater use of women's religious heritage in precolonial times as well as liberating elements in women's popular religiosity to find new symbols and language.

Jesus as a Priest of *Han*

The Korean context is quite different from that of the Philippines. Korea has never been colonized by a Western power, and Christianity did not arrive on the Korean shore with gunboats and canons. Instead, Korea, culturally and politically dominated by China for centuries, was colonized by Japan in the first half of the twentieth century. Korean feminist theologians have criticized Confucianism, Buddhism and Christianity as imported religions maintained by male elites, scholars, monks and priests, who help to sustain the patriarchal order in society. They have turned to shamanism, an ancient indigenous tradition that is still very influential today, for resources in constructing Christology. The majority of those who consult shamans are women, and female shamans exercise leadership and perform important healing roles.

In a recent article on 'Asian Christologies and People's Religions', Chung Hyun Kyung argues that theologians should shift their focus from institutional religions to people's religions, such as shamanism (1996: 214-27). She points out that institutional dogmatic religions are usually male-centered, power greedy and authoritarian, while people's religions are concrete expressions of their living faith and daily struggles. Yet she also cautions that not all elements in people's religions are liberating for women. Women are both agents changing popular religions as well as victims oppressed by these traditions. Thus, one should avoid romanticizing people's religions, while critically discerning their liberating as well as enslaving aspects.

Chung suggests four steps in constructing Christology, taking seriously the context of people's religions. The first step involves listening to people's stories of hunger, impoverishment and need. This means we should commit ourselves to the people's struggles as the beginning point of the process. The second step is a socio-political and religio-cultural analysis of why people are hungry and their lives diminished. In particular, this leads to a criticism of Christianity in terms of its relationship to

colonialism and neocolonialism as well as a recognition of the debilitat-
ing elements in inherited cultures and religions. The third step involves
the search for life-giving fragments and traditions. Inspired by Korean
minjung theology developed in the 1970s during the people's movement
against dictatorial regimes, Chung suggests the possibility of finding new
life-affirming meanings through the convergences of the Jesus story and
the stories of the people. This means that we pay attention to a 'non-
Christian reading of Jesus' in order to expand our theological horizons.
But to truly appreciate the people's stories, we must live in solidarity
with the poor and participate in grassroots movements. This step requires
profound humility and *metanoia* (conversion) of Christians, who often
assume that they alone know all the answers and true wisdom. The final
step involves actively building communities of resistance and hope to
sustain the struggle over the long haul and interpret Scripture and tradition from the perspective of the disfranchised.

Chung's methodology radically differs from traditional approaches to
theology in several ways. She suggests we listen to the people, instead of
turning to Scripture and dogma as our primary data and resource. She is
not preoccupied with past christological debates when they are not
relevant to the poor and suffering people of Asia in their struggle for the
fullness of life. She envisages the theological endeavor, not as a lonely
business, but as a collective activity, rooted in the integration of theory
and praxis. Most importantly, she attempts to break free from the narrow parameters set by institutional constraints, while constantly creating
new possibilities and seeking wider horizons.

Chung's four steps provide us with a framework to understand the
process through which she and other Korean feminist theologians
develop their Christology. Chung emphasizes the narrative nature of
theology and women's storytelling: 'The power of storytelling lies in its
embodied truth. Women talked about their concrete, historical life
experience and not about abstract, metaphysical concepts' (Chung 1990:
104). From these stories of the women and other oppressed people
emerges a powerful notion, *han*, that has become central to Korean
minjung theology. *Han* is a Korean word that expresses the deep feeling
that arises out of the experience of injustice. According to Kang Nam
Soon, '*han* designates the psychological phenomenon of people's suffering and is a feeling of the hopelessness of the oppressed, a feeling of just
indignation, or a feeling of unresolved resentment against unjustifiable
suffering' (Kang 1996: 134). She further observes that while the *han* of

minjung arises out of socio-political and economic oppression, the *han* of women mainly arises out of rigid sexual discriminations in Korean society.

When they are ridden with *han*, Korean women seek the help of shamans, the majority of whom are women from the lower-classes. The Korean shaman is a priest of *han*: through her powerful dances and rituals, she exorcizes *han* and restores the person's health, strength and hope. The release of *han* is called *han-pu-ri*, which usually involves three important steps: allowing the *han*-ridden person to speak and be heard, naming the sources of oppression and actively changing the unjust situation so that the person can have peace (Chung 1989: 143). While shamans usually deal with personal *han* and individual relief, those involved in political movements are rediscovering the potentials of shamanism to heal collective *han* and to channel the recovered energy for liberation.

Shamanism, as a religion dealing with *han*, has been condemned by missionaries as animistic and superstitious and despised by educated and Westernized Korean elites. But this women-centered religious stratum provides the language, the ritualistic practice and the imagination for some Korean feminists to describe their Christian experiences. In bringing the people's story and the Jesus story together, Chung speaks of *han* and *han-pu-ri*, instead of sin and salvation. Whereas sin connotes wrongdoing for which one is responsible, *han* captures the feeling of being *sinned against*, the helplessness of those who often cannot even control their own destiny. The dispersal of accumulated *han*, both personal and collective, restores the health and well-being of the individual and the community. Thus, Chung uses *han-pu-ri* to interpret Jesus' power to free others from injustice and suffering (Chung 1989: 145).

Among the pluralistic christological images proposed by Korean feminist theologians, Jesus is seen by some as a priest of *han*, a shaman who consoles the broken-hearted, heals the afflicted and restores wholeness through communication with the spirits. Korean women can relate to many stories in the gospels where Jesus' role resembles that of a shaman, exorcizing demons and healing the sick. Chung observes that: 'As the Korean shaman has been a healer, comforter, and counselor for Korean women, Jesus Christ healed and comforted women in his ministry' (Chung 1990: 66). Since the majority of their shamans are female, Chung states that Korean women connect more easily with female images of the Christ.

A female Christ is proposed also by Choi Man Ja, although not in a shamanistic context (Choi 1989: 174-80). Choi makes a distinction between the person of the Messiah and the praxis of messiahship. For her, messiah-praxis consists of Jesus' suffering as an outcast and his struggle to overcome oppression. Korean women, likewise, participate in the praxis of messiahship and are true disciples of Jesus. In other words, Korean women who are *han*-ridden and engage in *han-pu-ri* are 'the true praxis of messiah-Jesus'. Korean feminist theologians not only propose a female Christ, they have also organized a Women Church in Seoul, with a woman as priest and employing their own liturgies.

Although Jesus as a priest of *han* has been mentioned in several articles, Korean feminist theologians have not yet fully developed the notion. Future reflection needs to pay attention to the oppressive aspects of shamanism, such as its appropriation of the patriarchal elements of imported religions and its over-emphasis on the personal dimension of *han* (Lee 1994: 4-5). While *han* is a powerful term, Korean feminists debate whether women's *han* is different from men's as well as the appropriate strategies for exorcism. The reinterpretation of Jesus through the lens of shamanism requires a more in-depth biblical and historical exploration. Contemporary scholarship on the historical Jesus can shed much light on Jesus as a healer and a spirit-filled person. A more detailed exposition of the relationship between Jesus' life, ministry, and death and *han-pu-ri* needs to be spelled out. Moreover, what will be the impact of Jesus as the priest of *han* and other christological images developed by feminist theologians on the Korean churches, the majority of which are evangelical and conservative?

An Organic Model for Christology

Christianity has been brought into interaction with Chinese culture for many centuries, but the Christian population in China never exceeded one per cent until very recently. Moreover, there have been vehement anti-Christian movements in both the nineteenth and the early twentieth centuries. As a Chinese feminist theologian, I need to pay attention to the non-Christian perceptions of Christ among the Chinese before I reconstruct Christology. In recent years, I have explored christological images as a response to the growing ecological crises in China and other parts of Asia and as an attempt to dialogue with Chinese religions.

Because their millennia-old civilization has used characters (ideograms) for writing, the Chinese people have a linguistic structure, thought-pattern and worldview different from that in the West. The Christ figure, interpreted as the savior of humankind redeeming believers from sin and depravity, is quite foreign to Chinese thinking. Chinese culture has no equivalent concept of sin understood as human depravity in a religious sense, but it does include the concept of shame or guilt in a social sense. Moreover, Confucianism teaches that through studying the Chinese classics, self-cultivation and developing one's moral faculty, human beings can achieve moral perfection and sagehood. Likewise, Mahayana Buddhism, also influential in Chinese culture, emphasizes the capacity of all human beings to attain Buddhahood and the possibility of enlightenment (Kwok 1993: 24-32).

Some of the christological debates that have plagued the Christian West for centuries have little meaning in another cultural and linguistic medium. For example, the Chalcedonian controversy of whether Jesus is fully human or divine would not have taken place in China, which has a different philosophical system. The Chinese language has no verb 'to be' and has no equivalent word to convey the concept of being or essence. Thus, the debate on *homoousia* or *homoiousia* (whether the Son has the same substance with the Father or not) would be quite irrelevant to the Chinese people. Furthermore, the suffering of the Son on the cross to save the world is unintelligible to the average Chinese. In Confucianism, to have a son to continue the family line is a cardinal responsibility. That the Father would demand the death of the Son as a ransom or as a sacrifice would be unthinkable in the Confucian symbolic structure. Jesus as the sacrificial lamb is comprehensible only in the context of Jewish interpretation of sacrifice and atonement. For the Chinese, a gruesome disfigured Jesus on the cross suggests bad karma, disturbing the sensibility of harmony, peace and serenity in Chinese religiosity.

Attempting to bridge the mental gap between the East and the West and to create avenues for dialogue, I have to look beyond traditional anthropocentric images of Christ and atonement theories that depict Jesus as the ransom for humanity, the sacrificial lamb who expiatiates the sins of world, and the Son who satisfies the glory and honor of God. In Chinese cultural and religious thought, there is emphasis on the balance of heaven and earth, yang and ying, sun and moon, and father and mother. Instead of binary opposites, they are seen as complementary, mutually reinforcing and interplaying with one another. Thus, the predominantly androcentric images of Christ, such as Messiah, Lord, son of Man, son of God and king of Kings need to be challenged. The Chinese

religious worldview requires symbolizations of Christ using both feminine and masculine metaphors, images and concepts, such that women
and men can find their experiences reflected in the divine.

To develop a feminist ecological model for Christology, we have to
break through familiar images of Christ and dare to use non-human
metaphors. The nexus of sin and redemption must be rethought for sin
is more than the disobedience or egotism of human beings, but has a
cosmological dimension as well. People who live in traditional cultures
as well as indigenous peoples know intimately that their actions have
bearings on the natural environment, and not just on human history. An
ecological Christology will point to a vision of ecojustice for both
humans and nature and welcome the contributions of other religions
and traditions.

Moreover, christological understandings that easily lend support to
any forms of political and cultural imperialism must be debunked. The
militaristic and triumphant character of Christ during the Crusades and
Western expansion demonstrates how easily a religious symbol can be
coopted for political purposes. During the missionary movement, the
christological images missionaries fervently preached about were those
that justified Western political domination. Finally, the notion that Jesus
is unique, particular, and the only way to God must be demystified.
Such an exclusive understanding of Christ elevates Christianity above all
other religions, and has been used to justify conquest, colonization and
even genocide.

When we examine the plurality of images of Jesus in the New Testament, there are ample sources to reconstruct christologies using an
organic model (Kwok 1997: 113-25). Jesus uses the metaphor of the
vine and the branches to describe his relationship with the disciples (Jn
15.5). He refers to himself as the bread of life and the living water. He
also uses the feminine metaphor of a hen protecting her brood to
describe his passion and anguish for Jerusalem (Mt. 23.37). Coming
from a peasant background, Jesus frequently employs examples drawn
from nature in his parables and teachings. For example, God takes care
of the swallows and lilies in the field. The sun shines on both the good
and the bad. His nature sayings stress the universal love and provision of
God. One important aspect of his ministry is sharing table fellowship
with the people around him, even those who are despised, including tax
collectors and sinners. The messianic kingdom is referred to as a banquet
open to all. Jesus cares whether people have food to eat or not, as his

feeding the five thousand and other miracles clearly show. He has a profound understanding of ecojustice and challenges the Syrophoenician woman who belongs to the Greek-speaking urban class for exploiting the rural Galilee hinterland (Mk 7.24-30).

Besides recovering Jesus' organic metaphors to describe himself and the kingdom of God, another approach is to explore the image of Jesus as the wisdom of God. Feminist theologians Elisabeth Schüssler Fiorenza and Elizabeth A. Johnson have written on Jesus as Sophia-God (Schüssler Fiorenza 1994; Johnson 1993: 95-117). By the end of the first century, Jesus was seen not only as a wisdom teacher or as a prophet of Sophia, but as the incarnation of Sophia herself. The wisdom tradition in the Hebrew Bible highlights Wisdom's creative agency, providential power, redeeming capacity, immanence, and the promise of shalom, salvation and justice. Although the wisdom writings have not been accorded the same importance as the historical and prophetic books in the Bible, feminist theologians are recovering the cosmological emphasis in the wisdom tradition to address issues in ecological crises. Johnson, for example, writes: 'The use of wisdom categories to interpret Jesus had profound consequences. It enabled the fledgling Christian communities to attribute cosmic significance to the crucified Jesus, relating time to the creation and governance of the world' (Johnson 1993: 105).

It is important to note that the wisdom tradition has a broad, universal outlook on human history and is not so tied to the history and salvation of Israel alone. Jesus, seen as a wisdom teacher or as the personification of Sophia, creates new possibilities for dialogue with other ancient wisdom traditions in Asia. For example, Jesus' nature sayings in the gospels can be compared to the teachings in Confucianism that use natural symbols, such as the plant and the gardener, the cycle of seasons, and the stream and the water. Among the various images portrayed by contemporary Jesus studies is that of a *sage*, teaching subversive wisdom through proverbs, parables and aphorisms. The figure of the sage or teacher rings a bell in the Asian mind, much more so than the figures of the Messiah, the priest or the suffering servant. Although most of the Asian sages are male, such as Confucius and Gandhi, in popular Daoist and Buddhist traditions, women as well as men can be teachers passing wisdom from generation to generation. Jesus' teachings on ecojustice and his relations with the earth community around him can be compared to the cosmological teachings of the Asian sages.

Furthermore, an organic model of Christology relativizes the significance of Jesus as the revelation of God in a finite, historically specific, human form. Jesus, as the *epiphany* of God, is but one manifestation or revelation of the divine. The notion of an epiphanic Christ allows us to entertain the possibility of encountering Christ in many other ways: in other human beings, in nature, and in God's whole universe. This does not minimize the importance of the revelation of God in Jesus, because his life and ministry is paradigmatic for many Christians. But the incarnation of God can be also seen in both male and female salvific figures in other peoples' histories, who display great wisdom and compassion, and in forms of existence other than human, exceeding our shallow anthropocentrism. As I have written elsewhere:

> The Buddhist tradition asserts there is not one Buddha, but many Buddhas, and that everyone has the potential to attain Buddhahood. If we get away from the framework defined by a language of substance, we will not be fixated on a one-time incarnation. If we follow a non-dualistic logic, we can embrace the concept that Christ is one and many (Kwok 1997: 123).

To summarize, an organic model of Christology explores the implications of organic and natural metaphors for Christ, rediscovers the potential of wisdom Christology, and proposes to see Jesus as one ephiphany of God. It accents Jesus' teachings about right living, his relation with the natural environment and other human beings, his subversive wisdom on ecojustice, and his promise of God's compassion for all humankind. His death and passion are not singled out, but seen within the larger context of his struggle for justice for all—humans and all of creation. His resurrection can be seen as a rebirth, a regeneration that gives new hope. Sin is not so much human depravity or disobedience, but the breaking down of the interconnectedness of all things, threatening the web of life and the suffocation of mother earth. Sin is the systematic and structural evil that allows a tiny minority of the human race to use up the resources that exist for all. Sin is the power and the principalities that work against the oppressed, the majority of which are women and children, as well as indigenous peoples. Sin is the absence of love and compassion. It occurs when we close our ears and eyes to the cries of the people, the rivers and the trees. Sin is the brokenness that drives people to despair. Salvation, therefore, entails right relationship with one another, caring for the planet, compassion for the weaker links in the chain of life, while constantly remembering that humans beings are part of nature and the natural process.

Christ as the Embodiment of Feminine Principle

India is a land of vibrant spirituality, with temples and shrines at every corner, where people can offer flowers and incense. With a rich tradition of myths and legends, Indian people venerate a plurality of enchanting gods and goddesses. Colonized by the British for more than 150 years, India has been struggling with cultural identity, Hindu–Muslim strife, vast poverty and modernization since independence in 1947. Indian feminists have to fight not only against sexual discrimination but also the caste system, illiteracy and escalating violence against women.

The dowry system requires the bride's family to pay the bridegroom's family a certain sum of money. Women have been beaten, mistreated and even killed when the family fails to pay the dowry. Traditionally, women have been seen as the property of men, and the cruel tradition of sati demanded widows to show their loyalty to their husbands by being burned alive in the husband's funeral pyre. Indian feminist theologians have challenged these dehumanizing customs and expressed concerns over the plight of dalit (the untouchable) women. Indian women, they write, have been socialized to accept violence as their lot and self-sacrifice as virtue. Proverbs, such as 'Women, you should not weep when you are beaten', abound in Indian culture. Silent endurance causes women to suffer alone and to accept the curse of being born a woman. Those who protest and dare voice their criticism bring shame upon their families and are quickly censored and ostracized (Baltazar 1996b: 57). Instead of fighting injustice, many women helplessly accept their fate and look for consolation in reincarnation, in the life to come.

Given this cultural matrix, it is not surprising that Indian feminist theologians challenge the assumption that suffering is God–given, either for the perfection of souls or for the atonement of sin. Indian women are urged to suffer innocently for the expiatiation of the sin of others, for the well-being of their families, and for the long life of their husbands. Stella Baltazar, a Roman Catholic religious sister, objects to a patriarchal God who demands the suffering of the innocent to expiate people's sins:

> According to the dominant misinterpretation, this God demands the sacrifice of the innocent blood of the Son. God bestows wealth as a sign of favor, and poverty as a sign of curse, and gives rewards and punishments according to deeds. God delights in sacrifices and fasting but does not care about human beings (Baltazar 1996b: 59-60).

Her position echoes that of Rita Nakashima Brock, a Japanese American feminist theologian, who argues that the sacrifice of the Son by the Father is cosmic child abuse (Brock 1988: 56), and that the image of the innocent lamb reinforces the notion that victims ought to be innocent or virtuous or else suffering and pain are deserved.

Rejecting the images of the suffering servant, the silent lamb taken to slaughter, and the perfect sacrifice for the expiation of sin, Indian feminist theologians reclaim their cultural roots for resources to reconstruct Christology. They have attached importance to the Hindu concept of *Shakti*, the feminine principle which is the life energy of the universe. Aruna Gnanadason explains the meaning of *Shakti* as:

> the dynamic energy, which is the source and substance of all things, pervading everything. The manifestation of this primordial energy is called *Prakriti* (nature). Nature, both animate and inanimate, is thus an expression of *Shakti*, the feminine and creative principle of the cosmos; in conjunction with the masculine principle (*Purusha*), *Prakriti* creates the world (Gnanadason 1996: 75).

The concept of *Shakti*, the feminine and creative principle of the universe, is popularized by the writings of Indian eco-feminist Vandana Shiva. In *Staying Alive*, Shiva condemns modern science as a male project and development programs as the brain-children of Western patriarchy, leading to the death of the feminine principle. Citing statistics and field research, she argues persuasively that the degradation of women and the degradation of nature are intimately linked. She points to an alternative path for the survival of nature, women and men; and that path is characterized by honoring nature, sustainability and diversity. This is in sharp contrast to exploitation, consumption and surplus in capitalist patriarchy. For her, the feminine principle, or *Shakti*, is characterized by a harmonious relation between humans and nature, men and women, and the respect for diversity and the sharing of resources. Shiva celebrates the close links of nature and women as producers of life, and credits Third World women with playing an important role in providing sustenance for their families even under dire conditions. In recovering the chances for the survival of all life, she says, they are laying the foundations for the recovery of the feminine principle in nature and society and the recovery of earth as sustainer and provider (Shiva 1989).

In an attempt to reinterpret Christian faith through their religious heritage, Baltazar proposes seeing Jesus as an embodiment of *Shakti*:

The question for us is not to make Jesus become a woman. Rather, the transcended Christ can be the embodiment of the feminine principle, the Shakti, the energizer and vitalizer. It is a serious limitation to express the resurrected Christ in purely male or patriarchal terms. Only women can liberate him from this gross limitation. With his bodily death the maleness of Christ, too, dies. The risen Christ must be liberated from the violent male language, and this only women can do. Drawing from indigenous and primal religions, we need to make the resurrection of Christ become actual in our culture. In this way Indian culture, too, will experience a transformation by making alive an Indian cosmology of wholeness and interconnectedness which is truly the liberative potential of the cosmic Christ (Baltazar 1996: 64).

The embodiment of a principle in both female and male form does not seem to create difficulty in the Indian context. Avalokitesvara, the popular bodhisattva of compassion is venerated as a male figure in India, but called the Goddess of Mercy and assumes a female form in East Asia. There is also the half-female and half-male deity, Ardhanarisvara, who symbolizes mutuality and partnership of male and female principles and the union of human and divine. Thus, Baltazar finds it liberating to imagine God as both male and female, father and mother at the same time: 'The rediscovery of the feminine face of God ought to depict God as compassionate, life-giving, and life-sustaining potential, as the divine mother and father' (Baltazar 1996: 65).

The use of the philosophical and popular understanding of *Shakti* to interpret Christ has several advantages. It clearly links Christology to the emergent eco-feminist spirituality among Indian feminists. Christ, as the embodiment of *Shakti*, is the energizing force for harmony and interconnectedness of the whole cosmos. Instead of using Jewish or Greek male language to describe God, feminist theologians can reclaim their heritage and cultural roots to imagine the divine. It allows fruitful conversation and cross-fertilization among Christians such as Gnanadason and Baltazar and the Hindu Shiva. Furthermore, it recovers the feminine dimension of the divine, who is seen as supporting women in their struggle for freedom and humanity.

But there are cautions to the appropriation of Hindu concepts in Christian feminism. Indian male theologians have long tried to interpret Christian faith through the lens of Hinduism, without paying sufficient attention to the issue of sexual discrimination in the Hindu tradition. Feminist theologians, too, must critically examine the dualistic and hierarchical teachings in Hinduism, especially the rituals and taboos surrounding women. Otherwise, the recovery of the feminine principle will not effectively help women in their current struggle. In addition, the concept of *embodiment* must be fleshed out more fully. Why is it necessary for the feminine principle to be embodied and how is the embodiment in Jesus different from other possible embodiments? It will be interesting to compare and contrast the notions of Jesus as incarnation of Wisdom and Jesus as embodiment of *Shakti*.

The above discussion shows that Asian feminist theologians in various contexts have presented some fascinating ideas and approaches in their Christologies. They demonstrate that Asian Christian women can answer Jesus' question 'Who do you say that I am?' from their own experiences and circumstances. Some of them use anthropomorphic images to portray Christ; others opt for natural and cosmological metaphors. The question about the maleness of Christ does not concern them as much as in the West, since their cultures are full of gods and goddesses and do not prescribe that the salvific figure needs to be male. Many of them are aware of the limits of human language and metaphors to describe God and show remarkable capacity to hold duality together in unity—male and female, human and divine, cosmological and historical. Baltazar states that we should not limit God to any particular mode, because for her,

> God is multiple in communion.
> God is unity in diversity.
> God is universally local.
> God is transcendentally immanent (Baltazar 1996: 65).

Chapter Seven

Women and the Church

In the broader ecumenical view, new ways of being church extends to
and embraces all of creation and humanity in the whole inhabited world.
The church as a faith and human community is located in the midst of
the current global realities... Women become the prophetic voice as they
pose challenges to other women and men to repent and live the new
order of life.

Yong Tin Jin (Malaysia)

Although in many Asian churches women are the majority, they are
marginalized in the power structure of the church and the life of the
congregation. Colonial and patriarchal denominational polity reinforced
by indigenous biases and taboos against women has consigned them to
second-class membership in the faith community. Asian women's power
and authority are neither recognized nor respected by the male hierarchy of the church, or by those women who are steeped in the church's
androcentric teachings. Many churches have failed to live out the promise that women and men are full partners in the life and ministry of the
body of Christ.

At the same time, the increased participation of Asian women in the
economic and public sectors and the success of women's movements in
various countries have heightened the awareness of Christian women in
the local churches. They have grown increasingly vocal in rejecting the
misogynist teachings of the churches and patriarchal models of leadership. Advocating an equal partnership in God's ministry, women have
organized around numerous issues: the ordination of women, prophetic
roles for religious women, fuller participation of the laity in decision-
making processes and greater representation of women in church synods,
conventions and ecumenical gatherings. They argue that the church
must liberate itself from the bondage of sexism if it is to become a

prophetic voice in society and serve as a beacon of hope. For example, a group of women who participated in the Ecclesiology Consultation of the Christian Conference of Asia affirmed women's contribution to church life: 'The ideal Church enjoys koinonia (fellowship) in the true sense of the word. This ideal Church fellowship has women and men with equal partnership, it stands out as prophetic community committed for justice, peace and service with love'.[1]

Challenges to the Patriarchal Church

Many Asian feminist theologians lament the fact that churches in Asia are the products of their time, reflecting the patriarchal structures of society. Church women are often asked to fulfill stereotypical roles, such as keeping the altar clean, teaching religious education to children, helping in the kitchen or other secretarial and menial jobs. Religious women in some contexts are frequently asked to make the altar linens and vestments, care for the church buildings, provide for orphans and the homeless, teach catechism to children and play a subsidiary role to priests and bishops. In Roman Catholic circles, women are rarely asked to serve on consultative bodies for the bishops' conferences, participate in the decision-making process about vital issues of the church, help to lead the church in visible ways, and share in ministry and liturgy as equal partners (Lascano 1985–86: 12). The division of labor along gender lines in the churches regrettably reflects patriarchal realities found in many Asian societies.

The subordination of women in the church is due not only to misogyny within the Christian tradition but also to understandings of purity and taboo in respect to women in Asian religious traditions. For instance, Aiko Carter, a lay leader in the Japanese church, has observed that in Shinto religion, which emphasizes ceremonial purity, women's menstruation is seen as unclean and sexuality as negative. A similar negative attitude toward women is found in Buddhism, which requests menstruating women not to approach the altar. Further, women are often seen as hindering men's salvation, and thus impure and sinful. In some Buddhist traditions, women have to go through a rigorous spiritual discipline to become men in the next rebirth in order to be saved (Carter 1985–86: 34-35). Although in popular Buddhism and Daoism,

---

1.   CCA Ecclesiology Consultation Women Participants, 'Realities of the Asian Women in Society and Church', *In God's Image* (December 1986), pp. 5-7 (7).

women exercise certain leadership roles, including teaching the scriptures and founding new congregations, men feature more prominently
in the religious hierarchy and liturgical functions.

Instead of challenging these unjust social customs, congregations of
many Asian churches tend to perpetuate and reinforce male domination
through their teachings and practices. In the Roman Catholic Church,
the fact that Jesus was a male and that women do not resemble Jesus
physically are cited as reasons for barring women from ordination to the
priesthood. In many churches, Paul's injunctions that women should
not speak in church (1 Cor. 14.34-35) nor exercise authority over men
(1 Tim. 2.11-15) are used repeatedly to reinforce women's inferiority
and to deny them their rightful participation. Citing the Genesis story in
which Eve was created second but sinned first, some male pastors
reiterate their belief that women are sinful and dangerous and should be
under male supervision and control. The misogynist teachings in both
the Christian and indigenous traditions deny women equal opportunities
to serve and to lead.

The ordination of women to the priesthood is a protracted and
lengthy struggle in the Asian context. In some countries, various denominations are slowly opening to the possibility of ordaining women, but
some denominations still adamantly refuse to do so, even when women
have the training and the credentials. Women who serve as deacons or
evangelists do not receive the same recognition and benefits as ordained
ministers. Even when they are ordained, women generally receive less
pay than their male counterparts. Less likely to be called to large and
established congregations, they often have to start their own churches.
Female pastors employed as associates are assigned stereotypical jobs,
such as teaching the young, home-visitation, tending to the sick, and
responsibility for women's fellowships and outreach to women in
general. Married female evangelists and priests have the added difficulty
of having to negotiate between demands at home and in the workplace,
while single women working in churches are often viewed with suspicion, or even pity (see two surveys done in Korea and Hong Kong: Kim
1992: 10-18; Wong 1997: 13-16). Many female parishioners feel more
comfortable with men as their pastors and some are against women's
ordination, because they have internalized the churches' teachings of
male superiority.

Even in progressive Christian movements in Asia, men still dominate
the leadership and liturgical roles. For example, Lydia Lascano observes

that in basic Christian or ecclesial communities in the Philippines that are deeply involved in social justice movements, the majority of core leaders are men; when women leaders emerge, they are given tasks that are extensions of their usual functions of child-rearing and housekeeping (Lascano 1985–86: 12). In the Korean situation, progressive theologians organize *minjung* churches to serve those marginalized in society. Even though women are the *minjung* among the *minjung*, they often play a subordinate role in shaping the development of the *minjung* congregations.

Although there is an increasing number of women entering seminaries, the majority of faculty in theological schools in Asia are men. The theological curriculum in many schools follows that of seminaries in the West, with some adaptations to the local context. The kind of theology taught often reflects the mentality of middle-class, Western churches, instead of actively responding to urgent issues of the day or the pastoral needs of Asian people. Academic excellence is still defined largely by the ability to master the works of Western theological giants, such as Tillich, Barth, Rahner or Schillebeeckx. In such a theological climate, feminist theology is dismissed as not a serious theological discourse, or simply as a passing fashion of Western women and, therefore, irrelevant to Asian Christians. Few seminaries give priority to hiring more women and offering courses on feminist interpretation of the Bible, feminist theology and pastoral care that honors the dignity of women. Even when these courses are offered, they are likely to be electives and students are not required to take them to benefit from feminist theological insights.

If the churches are to carry out Jesus' mission in the world, many Asian feminist theologians contend, the current practices of sexual discrimination in church structure and theological education must be changed. Lily Kuo Wang, a Presbyterian minister in Taiwan, emphasizes the tradition of the church as the body of Christ, in which all members are mutually dependent, woven together through the power of love. Different parts of the body have different gifts and talents, and each should be encouraged to use its gifts to benefit the whole. In the Reformed tradition, Kuo believes in the priesthood of all believers and an inclusive ministry open to all. She insists that the church should be a living temple through which the love of God and the power of the spirit can be channeled. Women should become leaders and ministers of the church so that they can serve God fully and equally (Kuo 1989: 24-32).

Kuo's vision for an inclusive and mutually dependent church membership is shared by other Christian women leaders in Asia. For example, Esther Inayat of Pakistan challenges the church to provide more adequate theological training for women because such opportunities have been minimal in her country. Women are offered neither support nor encouragement when they decide to be involved in ministries of the church (Inayat 1989: 262-63). Nyunt Nyunt Thein writes that theologically trained women in Burma urge Christians to recognize that the structure of the church bars women from full ministries and to experiment with alternative models. At the same time, she points to the continued need to promote women's awareness and to develop feminist theological reflection. Critical dialogue and cooperation with women of other faiths, who are involved in promoting women's consciousness and status, should also be encouraged (Thein 1989: 271). Tan Yak Hwee of Singapore also implores the churches to give space for women to exercise their spiritual gifts and opportunities for equal participation in ministry. She believes the church should be liberated first before it can be an instrument of salvation for others:

> The Church must look upon itself as a community of people who have been liberated from sin, a redeemed people. It is Christ who gave them freedom for the purpose of serving others. With that understanding, the Church cannot but share this freedom among its members. A partnership of trust and commitment between men and women should be forged for the advancement of the gospel (Tan 1989: 276).

Discipleship of Women

In an effort to counteract the patriarchal biases of the churches, Asian feminist theologians search for examples of women's discipleship during the time of Jesus and in the early church. Virginia Fabella notes that women were among the followers who listened to Jesus' teaching and helped in his ministry, even though the 12 disciples were all male. For example, Luke 8 mentions that Mary Magdalene, Joanna, Susanna and others provided for Jesus and 'the twelve' out of their resources, as Jesus traveled through cities and villages with his followers. Touched and healed by Jesus women, such as Simon's mother-in-law, the hemorrhaging woman and the bent-over woman, witnessed to his healing power. Even Gentile women, such as the Samaritan woman in John 4, had the opportunity to listen to Jesus' teaching and spread his words in their communities. Most importantly, women were involved in the central mysteries of Jesus' life: in the Annunciation, the first miracle at Cana, the disclosure of Jesus as the Messiah, the death on the cross, and the Resurrection (Fabella *et al.* 1983: 12).

Focusing on women disciples of Jesus in the Gospel of Mark, Hisako Kinukawa elucidates the ways women follow Jesus' teaching of discipleship: 'If any want to become my followers, let them deny themselves and take up their cross and follow me' (Mk 8.34) (Kinukawa 1994: 90-106). Kinukawa argues that in Jesus' time the cross was a symbol of shame and to take up one's cross meant to stand on the side of the oppressed in society. True discipleship, then, requires one to model oneself on Jesus' life-giving ministries in solidarity with the outcast of society. Such a ministry may result in resistance and rejection, even suffering, execution and death. Another aspect of Jesus' teaching on discipleship involves serving: 'Whoever wants to be the first must be last of all and servant of all' (Mk 9.35). Kinukawa maintains that Jesus' teaching on service contradicts a power structure that seeks power at the expense of the destitute. By standing with the subjugated, Jesus set an example for discipleship, culminating in suffering and death.

Kinukawa then compares the male and female disciples in Mark's gospel. The male disciples argue who is the greatest and joggle for recognition and power. They flee when Jesus is persecuted, because they sense political danger and do not want to be identified with an accused criminal. In sharp contrast, Mark depicts the women disciples as following Jesus to the very end. Mary Magdalene, Mary the mother of James and Joses, and Salome follow Jesus to the cross, see where he is buried, and bring spices to anoint his body. At the beginning of the gospel, Mark describes Simon's mother-in-law serving Jesus after she is healed, and he concludes with the story of the women attending Jesus after his death. For Kinukawa, these women are true disciples:

> Thus, the women disciples keep challenging those who avoid joining the struggles of the oppressed. The women disciples continue to disturb churches that seek patriarchal honor and hierarchical authority. So it should be implied that the discipleship of 'following and serving' has the power to regenerate a true community of faith (1994: 106).

In addition to the exemplifying roles of the women disciples of Jesus, Asian feminist theologians point to the important ministries of women in the early church to argue for the fuller inclusion of women. Esther Inayat writes that women were baptized into full church membership. They participated in prayer groups and opened their houses for prayer

meetings and worship services. Women were also founders and sup-
porters of the early churches. They were prophets, evangelists and deaconesses working side by side with Paul and other male apostles (1989:
262). Tan Yak Hwee cites several women mentioned by name in the
New Testament as role models for contemporary women. They include
Dorcas, who did good works of charity at Joppa, especially for widows
in the church (Acts 9.36-42). In Ephesus, the couple Priscilla and Aquila
helped Paul spread the Gospel and in other missionary work. The fact
that Priscilla's name was mentioned before Aquila's signifies the respect
and importance of Priscilla's contribution to the early church (Acts
18.18, 26; Rom. 16.3). In the last chapter of the Epistle to the Romans,
Paul further expresses his appreciation for his fellow workers, including
Phoebe the deaconess, Mary, Tryphaena, Tryphosa and Persis. Tan concludes that these women played vital roles in the life of the early church
and their activities were not restricted to evangelizing other women.
The ministry of the church was not limited to men because both women
and men were called to follow Jesus, who came not to be served but to
serve (Tan 1989: 274).

Given the androcentric bias of the New Testament authors, Virginia
Fabella contends that the information given in the gospels and epistles
about women's ministry depicts only a fraction of reality. Citing the
work of Elisabeth Schüssler Fiorenza, Fabella argues that women participated in a discipleship of equals that existed for a period in early Christianity. She calls for a non-androcentric reconstruction of early church
history, which will reveal that 'women were full-fledged disciples, and
equally missionaries, prophets, church leaders, and apostles in the broad
sense of the term' (Fabella 1985–86: 5). Such re-examination will under-
line the egalitarian model of *ecclesia*, based on the equality of all Christians, male and female.

With other Asian feminist theologians, Fabella reclaims Mary, the
mother of Jesus, as a model of true discipleship. In the popular devotion
to Mary, she has been depicted as the new Eve, the perpetual virgin,
mother of God, mediatrix of grace, but seldom as 'disciple'. But in the
new perspective, Mary is seen as a woman with a profound historical
consciousness, sharing in her people's expectation of the coming kingdom of God. She is no longer an icon, far removed from reality, put on
a pedestal to be worshiped. Mary courageously accepts the challenge of
God to be co-creator of a new humanity at the Annunciation, breaking
the sexual taboo placed on women at her time. The Magnificat pro-

claims a profound message of liberation to people suffering under economic and political oppression. Mary participates in Jesus' ministry, follows him to the cross, and offers us a model of true servanthood. She identifies with mothers today whose children are persecuted and taken as political prisoners for their actions against injustice. The torture and death of Jesus do not frighten her, for she continues his ministry, meeting and praying with the disciples at Pentecost and helping to form the first church (Zambrano 1989: 222-27; Han 1989: 234-40). Fabella notes that Mary's special claim is not that she has given birth to Jesus, but she qualifies as a disciple and forms Jesus' family of disciples through her obedient response to God: 'Mary then remains a model for all Christians, not so much of motherhood, but of faith and discipleship' (Fabella 1985–86: 5).

For Asian feminist theologians, both women and men are called to follow Jesus and to participate in the ministry that brings about the kingdom of God. Like the women in the early church, contemporary Christian women seek to build an inclusive and egalitarian faith community. Like Mary, the mother of Jesus, they wish to respond to the challenge of God and participate in the co-creation of new humanity. True discipleship is not seeking power for one-self, but following Jesus and serving others for the sake of the kingdom. Asian women theologians have noticed that both the Christian church and the Asian traditions have exhorted women to serve in subservient roles. They insist that the true meaning of service is not perpetual denial of self, but radical commitment to bring about justice and the welfare of the church and society. Therefore, true discipleship of women does not perpetuate the male domination of church but liberates the hierarchical church and transforms it into a discipleship of equals.

Partnership of Equals

In the struggle for the equal partnership of women and men in the church, an analysis of power and authority and how they are exercised is necessary. Ranjini Rebera, a consultant in communications and a feminist theologian originally from Sri Lanka, has written on the nature of power and its impact on Asian women (Rebera 1997: 44-49). Authority, she says, is different from power. Authority is usually based on certain external circumstances, such as skill, knowledge, position or relationship. Power is much more complex and dynamic, having personal, social, institutional and religious dimensions. Rebera believes that power itself is neutral: it can be used for good or for evil, depending on how it is applied and for what purpose it is exercised.

Following feminist theologians, such as Rita Nakashima Brock, Rebera distinguishes two major models of power: power-over-others and power-with-others. Power-over is the power of domination and control. Within this model, an individual or a group of persons assumes control and dominance because of ethnic identity, class privilege, education, status or gender. In the Christian context, this hierarchical pyramid is supported by the belief that God is at the top, followed by the male, then the female, and then other categories of creation. The exercise of power is non-reciprocal, which often leads to an imbalance or even the abuse of dominant power. Whereas many men can exercise this power of domination because of their status and position, Rebera argues that some women also claim their right to control, based on their race or their husband's position of authority in the church or society, or based on their own position of authority within the women's movement. Insightfully she points out how women in subordinate positions also try to influence and control those in authority by indirect means and by creating dependent circles within the family, the church and community.

The other form of power is power-with-others, based on the interconnection that exists between all who share in a community. She says power-with-others can lead us on the journey to create 'a partnership of equals within the Community of Faith'. She elucidates several characteristics of power-with-others. First, it is rooted, not in a hierarchical model where authority is exercised from the top down, but in an egalitarian one where authority is communal and shared. Second, this model respects the difference and diversity of each member, giving voice and support to each one who is 'the other', who feels left out, silenced and abused. It allows openness and freedom for all to claim their cultural and religious identity. Third, power-with seeks justice for all who belong to the community. This implies the accountability of those who use power to control. It challenges authoritarian modes of leadership and unjust structures that create a power imbalance. It works to create community in which freedom, justice, peace and inclusivity prevail, instead of fear, separation, anxiety and alienation. Fourth, it offers an opportunity to transform our image of God from one who is omnipotent and dominating to one who is the source of life-giving power. Such a God creates each of us different but equal, and works in mutuality with human beings and creation.

Unfortunately, many churches in Asia operate according to a power-over model, with a top-down hierarchical structure. There is still a long way to go before the churches learn to exercise power-with so that all members can participate fully in the life of the church. A church that respects the discipleship of women and the partnership of equals has to rethink its patterns of leadership, the meaning of ministry, the mobilization of the laity and the relationship of the church and the community. The exercise of power must be dynamic, fluid, open and transparent. Mechanisms of accountability must be created and sustained so that power will neither be misused nor abused. Authority must not be based on position, credentials and status alone, but on charisma, the ability to build community and genuine qualities of leadership.

The clerical model of leadership that places power disproportionally on the clergy does not equip the laity to share ministry as full partners. In the Asian context where the culture honors the elderly, the teacher and the father of the household, the male clergy tend to act as patriarchs of an extended family, exercising power without appropriate mechanisms of checks and balances. The clergy is supposed to decide what is right and wrong, to represent the authority of God's Word and to dispense or withhold God's grace and absolution. The laity (especially the women among them) are to be obedient followers, consumers of religious goods and services, passive or even docile onlookers, restricted to the sidelines in God's messianic mission. In contrast, the model of a partnership of equals recognizes that all have a role to play in carrying out God's mission in the world. The clergy does not possess a more sacred status, but is called and set apart for particular functions. The laity must be equipped and encouraged to use their God-given talents to strengthen the church and to work for peace and justice in the community.

Asian feminist theologians who support women's ordination do not advocate a clerical-hierarchical model of the church. They do not support women's ordination so that women may have a fair share in the power of domination in the church hierarchy. They advocate women's ordination so that women who are called by God may have the freedom and opportunity to exercise power-with-others to equip the whole congregation. For them, the purpose of women's ordination is not to allow women admission into 'the male club' and the opportunity to perform 'men's roles'. They believe that women should not be contented with admission to the lowest rungs of church hierarchy, as deaconesses, evangelists, pastoral workers or priest associates. Instead, they envisage women seeking ordination to enlarge the church's vision of ministry, to experiment with new models of leadership and to subvert the patriarchal church.

Agatha Wong Mei-yuk of Hong Kong has noted that opponents to women's ordination often cite the following reasons for their opposition: (1) in the creation order, women are created after men and should play a subordinate role; (2) the husband is the head of the wife, and it is not appropriate for the wife to lead (Paul's injunction that women should not speak in church is often cited as support); (3) women by nature are not fit or suitable for the ministry; and (4) the tradition of the church does not provide for the ordination of women. Wong reminds us that there are in fact two creation stories in Genesis and in the first of these, the woman and the man were created simultaneously. The idea that women are subordinate in the natural order is a fiction maintained by a male system of control. Wong further points out that Paul's teachings are inconsistent. In Galatians he says that the redemption through Christ has abolished any distinction between races (Jew or Greek), classes (slave or free) and sexes (male or female). Meanwhile in the Epistle to the Corinthians, Paul exacts strict rules for women because of a controversy polarizing the troubled church. Paul's instructions must be understood in historical perspective because the human society has changed a great deal since Paul's time. Finally, Wong argues that the tradition of the church varies and changes over time. Jesus himself broke regulations of his time for the sake of justice and liberation (Wong 1989: 278-83).

Although Asian feminist theologians have tried to reinterpret biblical injunctions and church teachings against women, it will be a long time before the church can embrace the partnership of women and men as equals on personal, interpersonal, institutional and societal levels. For example, Gao Ying, a female pastor in Beijing, has noted that even though the socialist revolution has brought tremendous changes to China, ancient patriarchal attitudes toward women still exist. The church in China today is ruled primarily by the older generation of male leadership with the result that female pastors and church leaders are not treated as equals. From her own experience of working with those

women in her congregation who are searching for a positive identity
and self-esteem, Gao writes:

> Women's emancipation is an ongoing process and we certainly have a
> long way to go both to achieve greater leadership participation and part-
> nership equality. The liberation of the church women in post liberation
> China remains a 'Continuous Struggle' (Gao 1994: 59).

Continuous struggle lies ahead not only for women in the most
populous country in the world but also for women elsewhere in Asia. In
the past several years, the Ecumenical Decade of the Churches in Solidarity with Women has stimulated some churches to discuss the meaning of partnership, the admission of women to full ministry and the use
of inclusive language. Aruna Gnanadason, the director of the Sub-unit
on Women of the World Council of Churches, has been engaged in
numerous activities related to the Ecumenical Decade. She recalls that at
one Easter ecumenical gathering to launch the Decade in Madras, India,
the women asked the same question that the women disciples asked as
they approached the sealed tomb on that first Easter morning, 'Who will
roll the stone away?' The participants then responded, 'We will roll the
stone away' (Gnanadason 1992: 4). Assessing the achievements of the
Ecumenical Decade, it seems that many stones blocking Asian women
from full partnership in the church—and their hope for resurrection—
still need to be rolled away.

Hope for the Future Church

Although Asian Christian women face many obstacles in their struggle
for full participation in the ministry of the church, Asian feminist theologians express hope for the transformation of the church into a community of hope and justice. Some Asian Christian women, experiencing
ecumenical networks and local collaborative efforts, have had a foretaste
of what an inclusive faith community could be and have articulated
their visions of new ways of being a church in various contexts.

Yong Ting Jin of Malaysia points out two important metaphors for
the church found in the New Testament: the people of God and the
body of Christ. The term 'the people of God' has a long historical
Jewish background referring to the chosen people and a community
called to proclaim God's salvation for all humanity. The 'body of Christ'
refers to the church as a corporate life, in which members with a
plurality of gifts respect the contributions and dignity of one another.

The nature and character of the church can find its root model in the 'Jesus community' formed in the socio-cultural and political setting of Jesus' time. The 'Jesus community' was formed when Jesus announced the good news of God's kingdom as the new creation. The 'Jesus community' was a visible and dynamic sign of the kingdom oriented toward a radical transformation of the political and religious establishment of the time.

Translating the kingdom of God into social realities is the fundamental mission and challenge of the church in Yong's view. New ways of being church and women's participation are viewed from the perspective of God's kingdom and the new creation. Having served for several years as the Asian-Pacific secretary of the World Student Christian Federation, Yong has a broad ecumenical vision of the church as a dynamic movement, rather than a religious establishment coopted by the interests of the status quo. The church exists for the whole inhabited world, and women struggle together in solidarity as full members of the 'people of God, the body of Christ, new citizens of the kingdom, new creation made in God's image toward the vision of the New Heaven and New Earth where God's spirit, justice, peace, and love will reign and prevail in the order of life' (Yong 1989: 51).

In order for the church to serve as an agent ushering in the kingdom, Yong calls for the repentance of the church and a new life style in the religious community. Citing Brazilian theologian Leonardo Boff's analysis, Yong argues that the church has often abused or manipulated power, especially sacred power. Thus, a new way of exercising power and a new pattern of relationship between women and men on the personal and societal levels are necessary. Yong finds Jesus' exercise of power and authority out of deepest humility motivated by love and for service of others to be compelling example for the church to emulate:

> As a leader, Jesus washed the feet of his friends. This power is the blessing for one to live in love, in peace with justice, in community. This power is never violent or destructive, ego-centered or domineering. This power is understood, motivated, and exercised by one's set of values as patterned after the vision of God's new creation. It serves to foster, enhance, and nurture all of life. This power is dynamic and constructive because it has to do with caring, inclusiveness, peace with justice as against racism, sexism, classism, and militarism (Yong 1989: 49).

Yong's vision that the church exists not for itself, but for the wider human community is shared by Pauline Hensman of Sri Lanka (Hensman 1984: 19-23). Living in a country beset by poverty and ethnic strife between the Singhalese and the Tamils, Hensman believes that the arena in which the Holy Spirit operates is the whole world, and not just within the middle-class churches. She challenges the church to leave behind its colonial structure and its inherited privileges, which often create barriers between people instead of bringing them together. She anticipates an active laity not dependent on priests for leadership and for interpreting the Bible. Advocating for a decentralized church structure, she suggests that the minister should be socially involved outside the church and that the Holy Communion be celebrated in homes where committed Christians meet.

Hensman believes that the true ministry of the church is a kind of *missionary* ministry, not in the sense of converting 'heathens' to Christ, but of bringing the good news to the urban poor, the impoverished villagers and the over-worked laborers. She envisages the missionary-minister as working outside the parish churches, laboring side-by-side with workers and farmers on plantations and in factories and with prisoners and refugees. In this way, the missionary-minister can earn the trust of others and promote their awareness for the necessary action to bring about a new social order. The church will need many of these dedicated missionary-ministers with different gifts and insights to work among different people. It is in the context of a renewed ministry that Hensman hopes to see many women called to the ordained ministry. For her, women 'need to use fully the gifts and insights which God has given us women for leadership; to resist and triumph over male domination and sexism; for tact, sympathy, dedication and selflessness in God's service' (Hensman 1984: 23).

In another cultural context, Korean Christian women have gathered together and concretized their vision of an alternative model of the church by establishing in 1989 the Women Church in Seoul. The idea of Women Church was popularized through the works of Rosemary Radford Ruether and Elisabeth Schüssler Fiorenza, among others. The Greek word *ecclesia* is a political term, meaning the assembly of free citizens gathering to decide their spiritual and political affairs. An *ecclesia* of women, according to Schüssler Fiorenza, is 'the gathering of women as a free and decision-making assembly of God's people' (Schüssler-Fiorenza 1984: 349). The Women Church movement consists of grass-roots and ecumenical events and activities in North America and in other parts of the world. The Women Church in Seoul was established to share Christian concerns especially with the suffering women in

Korea and to work for the liberation of women from domestic and social oppression and for the healing of their *han* (Kwak 1992: 8-9).

The pastors of the Women Church in Korea have been ordained Korean women. Members of the Women Church creatively develop worship services and liturgies that are inclusive and adaptive to local customs. For example, instead of bread and wine for the Eucharist, they experimented with Korean rice cakes and ginger tea to symbolize Jesus eating with the poor and the lowly in their own setting. An important activity of the Women Church is feminist Bible study, because of the centrality of the Bible in Korean churches and spirituality. Using a participatory and dialogical style, the Bible studies introduce women to feminist and critical interpretations of the Bible. Monthly dramatizations of biblical passages helps members to understand more deeply the meaning of biblical stories. Other programs include counseling and healing sessions, collaborative work with local churches and other mission projects.

Although the Women Church is a small, struggling faith community in the midst of well-funded, patriarchal church establishment, it provides Korean Christian women with an alternative space and a forum where they can articulate their concerns and mobilize women for social transformation. A supporter of the Women Church, theologian Sun Ai Lee Park has shared her vision of the future church, modeled on the early Jesus community in which the human dignity of women and all others despised in society was realized. The future church must be free of sexism. It must strive to become a true community of women and men where the connection between women's oppression and other forms of injustice is recognized. Furthermore, the future church cannot be engrossed in middle-class concerns, but must become a grassroots movement. The forward-looking church should be a bearer of justice, engaging in the prophetic ministry of Jesus. Finally, the future church has to be a peace church, working for anti-militarization, anti-nuclear proliferation to usher in shalom on earth (Park 1989: 90-92). Today, women in the churches of Asia and throughout the world are called to be midwives giving birth to this future church in which everyone can participate equally as disciples.

Chapter Eight

Sexuality and Spirituality

We see the Spirit in the ancient gong
Calling us to silence, to listen
The embryonic rhythm of life
Vibrating, resounding, all-embracing

We see the Spirit in the water
Cleansing our body, healing our soul
We drink from the same cup
Renewing, sustaining, replenishing

We see the Spirit in the fire
Irrupting with passion, like a volcano
Our anger against injustice
Burning, glowing, fast-spreading

We see the Spirit in the circle
Learning Miriam's dance, taking first steps
In solidarity with all women
Dancing, chanting, spiraling

We see the Spirit in the colors
Taking pride in our culture, our rites
Black, yellow, brown, and white
Celebrating, living, rejoicing

We see the Spirit in our bonding
Confessing our brokenness, our division
Hope we offer to each other
Visioning, struggling, empowering

Kwok Pui-lan (Hong Kong)

The search for a passionate, life-giving and empowering spirituality has been a dominant theme in Asian women's theological reflection. The struggle against all forms of patriarchal oppression along with the celebration of women's strength and power have challenged stereotypical images of Asian women, defined by gentility, obedience and subservience. Our understanding of ways in which Asian Christian women are involved in personal and social transformation requires us to examine the form of Christian spirituality that focuses primarily on prayer, Bible study and other-worldly meditations. For Asian feminist theologians spirituality is not so much a gaze toward heaven or an emptying of the self, but rather the celebration of *ki* (the energy of life), the joy of living and the quest for wholeness.

Asian feminist theologians join other Third World theologians in the search for a form of spirituality that integrates body and soul, inner and outer worlds, and contemplation and social action. Specifically, they wish to reimagine and develop a spiritual practice that honors their embodied selves as women. All too often women's sensuality and sexuality have been regarded as lustful, dangerous and sinful, both in the Christian and in the Asian traditions. An embodied spirituality that affirms women's desire for love and their experiences as sexual beings allows women to feel at home with their bodies, with others and with God.

Women, Nature and Body

In 1974 Sherry B. Ortner published an important essay entitled 'Is Female to Male as Nature Is to Culture?' Arguing that female subordination is a universal phenomenon, she contends that there seems to be a common structure upheld in all human cultures: culture is valued more than nature and women are subordinate because they are seen as being closer to nature than men. Ortner's argument has influenced the framework of analysis of many Western feminist scholars in religion, who insist that both nature and women are subjugated under patriarchy. But Ortner's understanding of 'culture' as everywhere antagonistic to 'nature' is largely Eurocentric, influenced by Enlightenment thought and Western technological advances. Her observations can hardly be applicable in many Asian contexts.

Nature features prominently in the philosophical, moral and aesthetical imagination of many Asian traditions. Considered the highest ideal of spiritual quest for women and men, harmony with nature, a recurrent theme in Asian landscape paintings, is also evoked in poetry. While

Western feminists must either challenge the uneasy connection between women and nature, or reclaim positive dimensions of women's embodiment and their closeness to nature, Asian feminist theologians are faced with the glorification of nature in their cultures, while their own bodies are denigrated. To be born a woman, in some Asian traditions, is thought to be the result of bad karma or an indication of the lack of merit in previous lives. Female infanticide was widely practiced in traditional Asian societies and the selective abortion of female foetuses continues to be performed in China and elsewhere.

Exaltation of female symbols (including those of earth and nature) in Asian traditions does not necessarily lead to the valorization of women. The dynamic interplay between mutually inclusive and complementary yin and yang in East Asian philosophy has not been translated into a historical reality that honors women as equals. Because I have not found many efforts to explain this, I can only tentatively suggest some causes. As scholars in comparative religions have pointed out, the symbolic order of any given society may not be wholly symmetrical with the social order. Furthermore, female symbols of nature are usually restricted to the reproductive roles of women, such as fertility and nurturance; this in turn reinforces the domesticity of women. Thus the female symbols of the goddess, or the earth mother, may have been incorporated into the male symbolic structure, so that the symbolization of the feminine in connection with nature serves to keep women in their stereotypical roles.

Given this cultural background, Asian feminists do not need to reclaim the positive value of nature as do their Western counterparts. Their task is to reformulate the relationship between women and nature in such a way that women's embodied selves will be valued. They have known that the glorification of nature in Asian elite culture and the admiration of nature's aesthetic beauty do not lead to concern for the poor and oppressed, especially women who have to put food on the table. Instead of viewing nature in an abstract sense, Asian feminists see nature as the source of life and women's relationship with nature in terms of a political struggle for justice. Vandana Shiva lifts up Third World women's roles as creative managers of forests, the food chain, water resources and the livelihood of a household. These women also accumulate great knowledge of the environment because they have to learn to work with the most unyielding environments, the result of male migration from degraded rural areas. Shiva writes: 'The new insights provided by rural women in the Third World is that women and nature are associated not in passivity but in creativity and in the maintenance of life' (Shiva 1989: 47).

While some poor women in the Third World are creative managers of the environment, others have been forced to abuse the environment for the survival of themselves and their families. Aruna Gnanadason challenges Western feminists' romantic and often idealized picture of women's inherent connection with nature. In a more balanced and realistic analysis of women's roles in the ecological crisis, she remarks: 'While women are the worst inflicted by resource depletion, it is also true that because of forces they can scarcely understand, still less control, they are often the agents of their own resource depletion' (Gnanadason 1996: 76). Gnanadason is careful to note that while we should not blame the victims of our global economy who have to struggle to obtain even basic necessities, nor should we close our eyes to women's involvement in the destruction of nature.

In Asia when resources are scarce, women and girls have been told to take care of the needs of the male members of the household first, before attending to their own. The survival of male bodies is given priority because of the importance attached to the continuation of the blood line. In traditional Asia, women's bodies and sexuality were valued as long as women were able to produce male heirs and thus ensure the patrilineal line. In contemporary Asia, women's procreative power is not only controlled by her family but also by government regulations, in the name of monitoring population growth. In industrialized Asian countries, women's bodies are valued as cheap labor for national and multinational corporations, and women's sexuality becomes a commodity to be exchanged in the global market of sex tourism. Violence against women has not been considered an important crime and does not occupy the attention of law enforcement agencies. Further, some Asian countries lack adequate laws and policies to protect women against domestic violence and various forms of sexual harassment.

Women's bodies and normal female bodily functions are viewed with suspect and surrounded by taboos. For example, a Thai feminist journalist reports that:

> In everyday life, there are customs which attribute defilement to the female sex. A woman's clothes should not be washed together with those of a man; neither should they be hung in areas where a man might pass below. In either case, the man will lose his power, or spiritual superiority.

A truck that lets a woman climb up on the top is believed to be doomed.
She is of course generally not allowed to touch sacred Buddha images
(Hantrakul 1995: 227).

In another cultural context, women in Chinese society are regarded as
both ritually unclean and dangerously powerful, and they are barred
from certain activities in order not to inflict harm on others. Emily M.
Ahern discusses the different ways Chinese women are considered unclean and polluting:

> the first looks to the nature of allegedly unclean substances and their
> connection with birth and death; the second views the ascription of
> pollution to women as a reflection of their social role; and the third sees
> women's putative pollution as part of a system of ideas relating pollution
> to breaking the boundaries of social groups (1975: 193).

Such popular cultural and religious beliefs reinforce male domination
and inculcate in women and girls a sense of low esteem in respect to
their bodies and their selves. Some have willingly accepted a low social
status and unequal treatment as their fate and lot in life. Nantawan
Boonprasat Lewis, who is currently doing research on prostitution and
AIDS in Thailand, cautions that the internalization of such negative
images often paralyzes women, making them feel helpless and leading
them to a state of being 'willing victims'.

To challenge the dominant negative messages about women and
develop an ethic of feminist liberation, Lewis suggests self-redefinition,
self-rehabitation and self-acceptance as important steps. Women who
are survivors of oppressive systems, especially prostitutes who are treated
as social outcasts, have pointed to the power of self-redefination and
self-acceptance. They have challenged the social norms defining 'good'
and 'bad' women, and they have begun to see their bodies and sexuality
from new perspectives. Through naming reality in a new way, these
women have become moral agents of change, creating new possibilities
for themselves and their families. Lewis maintains that this self-trans-
formative process has a powerful spiritual dimension that must be
brought to the attention of the communities of faith, which need to
listen to women's stories and struggles (Lewis 1995: 228-29).

Chung Hyun Kyung also sees the healing of the body and the quest
for wholeness as crucial for Asian women. She says Asian feminists must
pay serious attention to the fact that many women's bodies are beaten,
torn, choked, burnt and dismembered. She challenges feminists to consider an 'epistemology from the broken body'. Asian women who have

become 'no-body' under the body-killing structures of foreign domination, state oppression, militarism and capitalism need to begin their
healing process by searching for ways to survive as human beings with a
sense of self-worth and purpose (Chung 1990: 39). Their bodies can
become whole again only when they can find means to exorcize their
han. The damage wrought by sexual exploitation and internalized oppression affects not only the physical body but the psyche and the spirit
as well. Therefore, the healing both of Asian women's broken bodies
and wounded spirits is important in a liberating and life-affirming spirituality.

A Wholistic View of Sexuality

Asian feminist theologians have pointed out that churches are not comfortable with human sexuality because sexuality has often been associated with sin, lust and worldliness. As the descendants of Eve, women
are seen as potential seductresses or temptresses, and their sexuality has
to be brought under the control of the patriarchal family or church. Sex
is restricted to marital relationships and there is a strong cult of virginity
and purity. Extra-marital relationships are condemned, and adultery,
especially when committed by a married woman, brings severe censor
and punishment from the community. Since matrimony is considered
ordained by God, there is little room for divorce or annulment of marriage, especially in the Roman Catholic tradition. Even when the husband becomes abusive, the wife is expected to suffer silently. Although
Asian cultures do exhibit diverse views on homosexuality, conservative
Asian churches have regarded homosexual relation as sinful and shame-
ful. The love between women, or lesbianism, is not seriously discussed
or is looked upon with scorn.

The narrow focus of the churches' sexual ethics and the degrading
attitudes toward women's sexuality have caused unspeakable pain and
raised barriers that prevent women's sexual expression. A group of
women who participated in the EATWOT consultation on 'Spirituality
for Life' called for a much broader understanding of the spectrum of
human sexuality:

> We need to construct a wholistic view of human sexuality. Sexuality
> encompasses one's total self-expression, relationship, and sensuality. Its
> development and practice should not be confined only in the context of
> marriage, but also in other unions and relationships where mutual respect,

commitment, and love exist. Viewing sexuality wholistically gives the
woman the option to marry someone or not, to be heterosexual or
homosexual, to have children or not, and to remain celibate or not
(EATWOT 1994: 131).

These women argued that sex and marriage enhance the growth of the
partners only when there is mutual and reciprocal commitment and
responsibility. Procreation should not be the main or only goal of marriage, and women's reproductive rights need to be respected. When a
relationship is no longer mutually life-giving, but rather destructive,
divorce or legal separation should be an option. More radical is their
view that sexual expression should not be limited to marriage, but
allowed also in other relationships where love and commitment exist.
They urged further that in wedding ceremonies, symbols, rituals and
words that suggest unequal power between wife and husband be aban-
doned and replaced by those that encourage mutuality and equality.

Instead of regarding sexuality as sinful and dirty, some Asian feminist
theologians embrace it as one of God's gifts to humanity. Elizabeth
Dominguez, a respected Filipino scholar of Hebrew Scriptures, uses the
creation stories in Genesis to illustrate the biblical understanding of
sexuality. In ch. 1, she observes, male and female are created in the
image of God (1.26-28). She thinks it distorts the meaning of human
sexuality to regard the 'image of God' as the specific qualities of individual persons rather than a way of living with one another. It is through
having fellowship together, and in mutual acceptance of one another,
that human beings reflect the glory and image of God. In Genesis 2,
Dominguez notes that when Eve is created, the Scripture says 'a man
leaves his father and his mother and clings to his wife' (2.24). Sex is
God's provision for the deepest communion between humans, which
can only take place if it is a communion between equals. She writes:
'Sexuality therefore is a gift of God for highest communion of human
beings' (Dominguez 1989: 85). She also notes that the Song of Songs
is a collection of erotic poetry that celebrates sexuality as God's gift.
Unfortunately the book has been interpreted allegorically both in the
Jewish tradition and in Christian heritage, so that its original meaning is
almost lost. The book evokes the beauty of human sexuality and claims
that erotic love is in the 'very plan of God' (Dominguez 1989: 86).

Asian feminist theologians affirm women's sensuality and sexuality as
integral and important parts of their spirituality. They reject the dualistic
and Platonic view of the mind as superior to the body, and the Pauline

teaching of the spirit in conflict with the flesh. A woman's yearning for union with others does not interfere with her longing and desire for God. Instead of being self-denying, focused on the suppression of women's desire, women's spirituality should be liberative and passionate, freeing women to be in touch with themselves and with others. Mary John Mananzan has articulated such a spirituality with poetic eloquence:

> It is holistic rather than dualistic. It is risk rather than security. It is a spirituality that is joyful rather than austere, active rather than passive, expansive rather than limiting. It celebrates more than it fasts; it lets go rather than holds back. It is an Easter rather than a Good Friday spirituality. It is vibrant, liberating, and colorful (Mananzan 1989: 112).

Such an active and spontaneous spirituality does not seek an escape from women's embodied selves or a repression of women's dynamic erotic energy. Asian feminist theologians remember that in the tradition of female mystics, women's intimate longing for God has often been portrayed by erotic and sexual imagery. The intimate language of erotic desire to be in communion with another becomes the medium for conveying the vulnerability, ambiguity and risk that women experience in God's presence.

Women's love and longing are not directed solely to men, but to other women as well. Lesbian love has been for some time a taboo subject, not only in Asian churches but also in Asian feminist theology. Recently, however, feminist theologians in Asia have become more outspoken on the issue of the diverse sexual orientations of women. Chung Hyun Kyung has explained why the love between women is forbidden in a patriarchal society. She says women have been raised to serve men's interests and needs. They are objects of men's sexual desire and pleasure and not subjects of their own destiny and relationships. They are trained to develop intimate relationships with men only and not to cultivate life-affirming relationships with other women. Separated and isolated within the patriarchal system, women are often jealous of one another. They compete for men's favor because their self-worth can only be affirmed by men (Chung 1988: 68).

For Chung, women need to learn to love and respect one another in order to successfully challenge the patriarchal system and to sustain the feminist movement. She says: 'If Asian women's changing relationships with their primary partners is a sign of self-awakened and self-affirming women in their personal lives, then the organized women's movement in solidarity with the larger people's movement for justice is a sign of

Asian women's self-love in public life' (Chung 1990: 46–47). Dominguez points to biblical models for women's love for one another. The story of Ruth and Naomi, for example, shows a remarkable relationship of unreserved sharing of love. On homosexuality, Dominguez is bold to say:

> I think if homosexuality has to be condemned, it has to be condemned only on the grounds that persons are degraded… If homosexuality prevails in our society, perhaps it is because heterosexual relationships are being exhausted because of the kind of society we are in, no longer being able to give human caring that human beings need…what I am saying is to judge that homosexuals are violating the law of God is, I think, a case of being culturally determined by the Scripture (Dominguez 1983: 9).

The small number of lesbians who are Christians often find themselves ostracized by both the Asian churches and by the mainstream women's movement, which does not want to risk being labeled as a lesbian movement. But some lesbians have begun to organize themselves and come out of the closet. In Hong Kong, a group of Christian lesbians and gay men formed the Ten Percent Club, which has sponsored forums on sexuality and organized alternative worship services. They also network with other gay and lesbian organizations in Asia and other parts of the world. The Ten Percent Club has issued an 'Homosexual Declaration', modeled on the Apostles' Creed:

> I believe in God,
> God created human beings in God's image.
> God was pleased with what God has created, including
> homosexuality and heterosexuality.
> God's kindness and righteousness grant us the rights of
> equality—the right to love and to be loved.
> I believe in my Savior Jesus Christ;
> His sacrifice redeemed us. He came to earth to save the ones who were
> being oppressed and being discriminated against.
> We deeply believe that He loves homosexuals as well. So we can serve
> others who have the same needs through His love.
>
> I believe in the Holy Spirit;
> She makes me witness to the Lord's immense love and glory.
> She lives among us to prove that homosexuals are also
> members of the Lord's family.
> When the Day comes, we can earn the crown and glory like
> other Christians.

I believe in the Church of holiness and righteousness,
the Church of reconciliation,
the Church where people love one another,
the Church that accepts different sexual orientations.
Amen (Ten Percent Club 1997: 49).

Spirituality for Life

Asian feminist theologians have critiqued a disembodied spirituality that
focuses on the personal life of prayer and meditation, looking for
rewards in heaven. They speak instead of a spirituality that is communal,
life-affirming, eco-conscious, one that empowers women in their
struggles. This is a spirituality for life, which celebrates the power of
women to give birth to life, to nurture and build justice and to reverse
the patriarchal history of death. It celebrates life in its fullness and cares
especially for those species that are endangered. It sustains the dreams
and aspirations of women and men who work for the dawn of a new
civilization, characterized by reciprocity, sustainability and interconnection.

Commitment to a spirituality for life calls for fundamental transformation in our spiritual orientation, as Chung Hyun Kyung points out
in her address to the Assembly of the World Council of Churches. First,
she urges for a change from anthropocentrism to life-centrism, recognizing that human beings are a small part of the universe and have to
learn to live in harmony with the earth and all its creatures. Second, she
calls for a change from the habit of dualism to a habit of interconnection. Dualism has exerted lasting influences in the Christian tradition
and has shaped the assumptions upon which social orders are constructed. Dualism leads to division, separation and the domination of
one group over others. Human beings need to live not with dividing
dualism but with integration of the interconnectedness of all beings.
Third, she envisions the change from the 'culture of death' to the 'culture of life'. By 'culture of life' she means the work for peace, for a just
political economy and for a healthy environment for all (Chung 1991:
43-46).

Many Asian feminist theologians share Chung's emphasis on a life-
centered and cosmic spirituality that does not elevate human beings
above the rest of creation. Some have looked to indigenous traditions
for wisdom, where the natural is not separated from the cultural and the
spiritual. In tribal communities, nature is not glorified or romanticized as

in Asian elite cultures, but rather it is regarded as the foundation of life. Women in these tribal communities seem to enjoy much more power and privileges than in other societies. Victoria Tauli-Corpuz, who comes from the tribal community of the Igorots in northern Luzon, the Philippines, describes her heritage in this way:

> Nature to the indigenous women and men is thought of in spiritual terms. In spite of the aggressive Christianization drive among the Igorots, the majority are still animist in orientation and practice. Nature spirits are revered, respected and feared. Rituals are done to thank or appease nature spirits and ancestors (Tauli-Corpuz 1996b: 100).

Tauli-Corpuz characterizes the indigenous spirituality as earth-based, with rituals coinciding with agricultural cycles and the life-cycles. Celebrations and rituals are performed before planting and harvesting rice, during births, weddings, deaths and at other such times. Also, the ideal of harmony with nature is closely related to the interdependence of the community. For example, the ancestral land is to be shared for the sustenance and life of the whole community. There is no wide gap between rich and poor in tribal communities because the principles of sharing and interdependence prevail. While Westernization and modernization are considered irresistible forces of history, she believes that indigenous traditions have much to offer to our contemporary quest for life-giving spirituality: 'The basic values of unity, sharing and interdependence, democracy and consensual decision-making, collectivity and integrity undergird Igorot women's spirituality' (Tauli-Corpuz 1996: 102).

Eco-centered feminist spirituality is gaining momentum in other parts of Asia, particularly on the Indian subcontinent. The Chipko movement, a women's grassroots drive to save the forests of India for food and fuel for their poor communities, has inspired the imagination of Indian feminist theologians. The word *chipko* means to hug or to embrace. The Chipko movement dates back three hundred years to a time when members of the Bishnoi community led by a woman, Amrita Devi, attempted to save their sacred Khejri trees by clinging to them. For Aruna Gnanadason, the Chipko movement symbolizes women's struggle for life, whether it is hugging trees, protesting against nuclear installations, participating in reforestation programs or boycotting the construction of dams in the Narmada Valley. In the Indian religious worldview, *Shakti* is the feminine and creative principle of the universe. In pleading for an eco-centered view and in demanding a greater sensitivity and respect of life, women are evoking this feminine principle, which is the source of all life forms (Gnanadason 1996: 75).

Several qualities characterize this eco-centered feminist spirituality. First, this spirituality is not other-worldly, private and abstract, rather it is forged in the experiences of communal struggle against oppression and injustice. Such struggle is based on women's growing awareness of their subordinate role imposed by a patriarchal society and their negative self-image resulting from the internalization of the dominant society's messages. Working with other women, they discover the power of solidarity, female bonding and sisterhood. Celebrating victories, large or small, they learn to exert their power as subjects of history and agents of social change. Confronting the global economy dictated by profit and greed, they attempt to articulate an alternative vision of communal sharing and survival for all. Such experiences enable women to encounter the power of the Spirit in both personal and societal transformation, leading them to think about spirituality in new ways. Mary John Mananzan notes: 'Women's emerging spirituality is therefore not just a vertical relationship with God but an integral one. It is shaped not only by prayer but by relational experience and struggle, personal, interpersonal, and societal' (Mananzan 1989: 112).

Second, an eco-centered feminist spirituality does not separate social action from contemplation. In the Philippines, for example, some activists are reclaiming the contemplative traditions of Asian religions. Some have taken up Zen Buddhist practices to learn to release the energy from the superactive mind and to achieve an inner balance and harmony. Through attention to breathing and other meditative exercises, they hope to be more attuned to nature and to be at one with the Breath of God. Other religious women have appropriated elements of Taiji, a martial art form from China, to develop spiritual practices that facilitate the healing of the body and the mind. In Sri Lanka, Christian feminists have joined together with Buddhists in dialogue to discover a common wisdom in the pursuit of a wholistic spirituality. A group of Indian theologians explain the interconnection between contemplation and action in this way:

> Contemplation is an aspect of openness, be it contemplation of nature or of history, be this biblical history or contemporary history... Contemplation may, in fact it must, deepen into probing and analysis of social reality with a view to finer response. If openness is a first response and contemplation, its continuation to action is its culmination (Indian Preparatory Group 1992: 76-77).

Third, an eco-centered feminist spirituality challenges insatiable con-sumerism and the obsessive gratification of material needs. The mass media has popularized the idea that possession of material goods is essen-tial to a good life, and the global economy has promoted a homogenous consumption pattern modeled after the West's. Such powerful ideolo-gies work against the long cherished practices of voluntary poverty and simplicity of life in Asian spirituality. Many Asian people, especially the younger generation, have become ardent worshipers of Mammon, cast-ing aside their spiritual heritages. Asian feminist theologians call for a radical shift in a developmental pattern modeled after the West. They urge others to cultivate a reconnection with a more wholistic, healthy, simple life style that saves wastes and respects the integrity of the earth.

Fourth, such a spirituality encourages and celebrates the diversity and plurality of experiences. It recognizes that uniformity and homogeniza-tion often suppress women's freedom and creativity to meet their own spiritual needs. Indigenous women and minority groups are often for-cibly assimilated into the larger society, compelled to give up local tradi-tions and expressions. A creative spirituality will encourage women to experiment with diverse cultural forms, to develop their gifts, to explore cultural hybridization and to transgress boundaries set by the status quo. The celebration of plurality will transform the liturgy and the life of the congregation, including the use of inclusive language, the partnership of women and men in ministry, a reorientation of religious and theological education, and a spirituality that is sensitive to both biological and cul-tural diversity.

I would like to summarize Asian women's emerging spirituality with the following:

> Women's attempts to break through the culture of silence and to trans-form their pain into political power are a deeply spiritual experience. The attempts to draw on creative expressions—dance, drama, poetry, music, art, story-telling and folklore—to give expression to the new-found con-sciousness and energy is spirituality. The longing to reclaim their femi-ninity, as they would define it, and to reclaim their right to control their own reproductive capabilities is spirituality. It is a spirituality that would say 'yes' to life and 'no' to forces of death (Indian Preparatory Group 1992: 71).

Bibliography

Editorial
    1993   'East Asian Miracle', *Far Eastern Economic Review* (21 October 1993): 5.

Abraham, Dulcie
    1986   'Set Free', in Women's Concerns Unit, Christian Conference of Asia (ed.), *Reading the Bible as Asian Women* (Singapore: Christian Conference of Asia): 78.
    1989   'Feminine Images of God', *In God's Image* (June): 3-7.

Abraham, Dulcie *et al.* (eds.)
    1989a   *Asian Women Doing Theology: Report from Singapore Conference, November 20-29, 1987* (Hong Kong: Asian Women's Resource Center for Culture and Theology [AWRC]).
    1989b   *Faith Renewed: A Report on the First Asian Women's Consultation on Interfaith Dialogue* (Hong Kong: AWRC).

Ahern, Emily M.
    1975   'The Power and Pollution of Chinese Women' in Margery Wolf and Roxane Witke (eds.), *Women in Chinese Society* (Stanford: Stanford University Press): 193-214.

Ahn, Sang Nim
    1989   'Feminist Theology in the Korean Church', in Fabella and Park (eds.): 127-34.

Antone, Hope S., and Yong Tin Jin (eds.)
    1992   *Re-Living Our Faith Today: A Bible Study Resource Book* (Hong Kong: World Student Christian Federation, Asia-Pacific Region).

AWRC
    1991   *Faith Renewed*. II. *A Report on the Second Asian Women's Consultation on Interfaith Dialogue, November 1–7, 1991, Columbo, Sri Lanka* (Seoul: AWRC).
    1997   *Women in the New Creation* (Kuala Lumpur: AWRC).

Azariah, Khushnud *et al.*
    1989   'Who Will Move the Stone?' *In God's Image* (June): 48-49.

Baltazar, Stella
    1996   'Domestic Violence in Indian Perspective', in Mananzan *et al.* (eds.): 56-65.

Battung, Rosario
    1993   'Women of Compassion: A Filipino Image of Mary', *In God's Image* 12.3: 42-47.

Bell, Derrick
    1992   *Faces at the Bottom of the Well: The Permanence of Racism* (New York: Basic Books).

Brock, Rita Nakashima
    1988   *Journey By Heart: A Christology of Erotic Power* (New York: Crossroad).

Brock, Rita Nakashima, and Susan Brooks Thistlethwaite
    1996   *Casting Stones: Prostitution and Liberation in Asia and the United States* (Minneapolis: Fortress Press).

Bultmann, Rudolf
    1956   *Primitive Christianity in its Contemporary Setting* (London: Thames and Hudson).

Carter, Aiko
    1985–86   'Women in Church and Society—a Japanese Perspective', *In God's Image* (December 1985-February 1986): 34-36.

Chan, Wing-tsit
    1969   *A Source Book in Chinese Philosophy* (trans. and comp.; Princeton: Princeton University Press).

Chang Sang
    1986   'Mission and Competence of Church Women in Korea', *In God's Image* (December 1985–February 1986): 42-48.

Cho, Wha Soon
    1988   *Let the Weak Be Strong* (Bloomington: Meyer Stone Books).

Choi, Man Ja
    1989   'Feminist Christology', in Abraham *et al.* (eds.) 1989a: 174-80.
    1991   'A Feminist Theology of the Korean Goddesses', in AWRC (1991): 180-90.

Chopp, Rebecca
    1996   'Eve's Knowing: Feminist Theology's Resistance to Malestream Epistemological Frameworks', in Elisabeth Schüssler Fiorenza and Mary Shawn Copeland (eds.), *Concilium 1996/1: Feminist Theologies in Different Contexts* (Maryknoll, NY: Orbis Books): 116-23.

Christ, Carol P.
    1997   *Rebirth of the Goddess: Finding Meaning in Feminist Spirituality* (Reading, MA: Addison-Wesley Publication Co.).

Chung Hyun Kyung
    1988   'Following Naked Dancing and Long Dreaming', in Letty Russell *et al.* (eds.), *Inheriting Our Mothers' Gardens: Feminist Theology in Third World Perspective* (Louisville: Westminster Press): 54-72.
    1989   ' "Han-pu-ri": Doing Theology from Korean Women's Perspective', in Fabella and Park (eds.): 135-46.
    1990   *Struggle to Be the Sun Again: Introducing Asian Women's Theology* (Maryknoll, NY: Orbis Books).
    1991   'Come, Holy Spirit—Renew the Whole Creation', in Michael Kinnamon (ed.), *Signs of the Spirit, Official Report, Seventh Assembly* (Geneva: World Council of Churches): 37-47.
    1996a   'Asian Christologies and People's Religions', *Voices from the Third World* 19.1: 214-27.
    1996b   'Your Comfort Vs My Death', in Mananzan *et al.* (eds.) 1996: 129-140.

Chung, Lee Oo
    1988   'Bible Study on Peace and Unification', *In God's Image* (June): 24-28.
Crescy, John *et al.*
    1988   'The Exodus Story', *In God's Image* (September): 43-48.
Dalai Lama (fourteenth)
    1979   *Aryashura's Aspiration and a Meditation on Compassion* (trans. T. Gyatso; Dharamsala: Library of Tibetan Works and Archives).
Daly, Mary
    1973   *Beyond God the Father: Toward a Philosophy of Women's Liberation* (Boston: Beacon Press).
    1978   *Gyn/Ecology: The Metaethics of Radical Feminism* (Boston: Beacon Press).
Dominguez, Elizabeth G.
    1983   'A Continuing Challenge for Women's Ministry', *In God's Image* (August 1983): 7-9.
    1989   'Biblical Concept of Human Sexuality: Challenge to Tourism', in Fabella and Park (eds.): 83-91.
EATWOT Women's Commission
    1985   *Proceedings: Asian Women's Consultation, Manila, 21–30 November, 1985* (Manila: Ecumenical Association of Third World Theologians).
    1994   *EATWOT Asian Women's Consultation: Spirituality for Life: Women Struggling against Violence* (Madaluyong, the Philippines: Ecumenical Association of Third World Theologians).
Fabella, Virginia
    1985–86 'Mission of Women in the Church in Asia: Role and Position', *In God's Image* (December 1985–February 1986): 4-9.
    1988   'A Common Methodology for Diverse Christologies?' in Fabella and Oduyuye (eds.): 108-17.
    1993   *Beyond Bonding: A Third World Women's Theological Journey* (Manila: Ecumenical Association of Third World Theologians).
Fabella, Virginia *et al.*
    1983   'Woman and the Church—It's the Men's Problem', *In God's Image* (April): 11-12.
Fabella, Virginia, and Mercy Amba Oduyoye (eds.)
    1988   *With Passion and Compassion: Third World Women Doing Theology* (Maryknoll, NY: Orbis Books).
Fabella, Virginia, Peter K.H. Lee and David K.S. Suh (eds.)
    1992   *Asian Christian Spirituality: Reclaiming Traditions* (Maryknoll, NY: Orbis Books).
Fabella, Virginia, and Sun Ai Lee Park (eds.)
    1989   *We Dare to Dream: Doing Theology as Asian Women* (Maryknoll, NY: Orbis Books).
Faria, Stella
    1988   'On Language and Sexism', *In God's Image* (December): 52-55.
    1989   'Feminine Images of God in Our Traditional Religions', *In God's Image* (June): 7-17.
Fernando, Chitra
    1986   'Women and Racism, I', in Women's Concerns Unit, Christian Conference of Asia (ed.) 1986: 41-46.

Gao, Ying
    1994   'The Place of Women in the Church in China', *In God's Image* 13.4: 56-60.
Gilmartin, Christina K. *et al.* (eds.)
    1994   *Engendering China: Women, Culture and the State* (Cambridge, MA: Harvard University Press).
Gnanadason, Aruna
    1988   'Feminist Theology: An Indian Perspective', *In God's Image* (December): 44-51.
    1992   'The Ecumenical Decade of the Churches in Solidarity with Women', *Church and Society* 82: 4-14.
    1993   *No Longer a Secret: The Church and Violence against Women* (Geneva: World Council of Churches).
    1996   'Toward a Feminist Eco-Theology for India', in Rosemary Radford Ruether (ed.), *Women Healing Earth* (Maryknoll, NY: Orbis Books): 74-81.
Gnanadason, Aruna (ed.)
    1986   *Towards a Theology of Humanhood: Women's Perspectives* (Delhi: All India Council of Christian Women).
Goldstein, Valerie Saiving
    1960   'The Human Condition: A Feminine View', *Journal of Religion* 40: 100-12.
Gross, Rita M.
    1996   *Feminism and Religion: An Introduction* (Boston: Beacon Press).
Hall, Stuart
    1990   'Cultural Identity and Diaspora', in Jonathan Rutherford (ed.), *Identity: Community, Culture, Difference* (London: Lawrence and Wishart): 222-37.
    1996a   'When Was "The Post-Colonial"? Thinking at the Limit', in Iain Chambers and Lidia Curti (eds.), *The Post-Colonial Question: Common Skies, Divided Horizon* (London: Routledge): 242-60.
    1996b   *Critical Dialogues in Cultural Studies* (ed. David Morley and Kuan-hsing Chen; London: Routledge).
Han, Yuk Yom
    1989   'Mariology as a Base for Feminist Liberation Theology', in Abraham *et al.* (eds.) 1989a: 234-40.
Hantrakul, Sukanya
    1995   'Prostitution in Thailand', unpublished paper quoted in Nantawan Boonprasat Lewis, 'Toward an Ethic of Feminist Liberation and Empowerment: A Case Study of Prostitution in Thailand', in Shin Chiba *et al.* (eds.), *Christian Ethics in Ecumenical Context* (Grand Rapids: Eerdmans): 219-30.
Hensman, Pauline
    1984   'Towards the Acceptance of Women's Total Participation in the Ministry', *In God's Image* (April): 19-23.
    1985   'Mary Speaks', *In God's Image* (October): 24-26.
Huntington, Samuel P.
    1996   *The Clash of Civilizations and the Remaking of World Order* (New York: Simon & Schuster).
Inayat, Esther
    1988   'Miriam', *In God's Image* (December 1987–March 1988): 29-30.

1989   'Ecclesiology and Women: A Biblical Perspective', in Abraham *et al.* (eds.)
            1989a: 257-65.
1992   'Hannah: A Woman of Strong Faith', in Lee Oo Chung *et al.* (ed.),
            Women of Courage: Asian Women Reading the Bible (Seoul: AWRC): 85-92.
Indian Preparatory Group
1992   'An Indian Search for a Spirituality of Liberation', in Fabella, Lee and Suk
            (eds.): 64-84.
Jayawardena, Kumari,
1986   *Feminism and Nationalism in the Third World* (London: Zed Books).
John, Crescy *et al.*
1988   'The Exodus Story', *In God's Image* (September): 43-48.
Johnson, Elizabeth A.
1993   'Wisdom Was Made Flesh and Pitched Her Tent among Us', in Maryanne
            Stevens (ed.), *Reconstructing the Christ Symbol* (New York: Paulist): 95-117.
Kang, Nam-Soon
1995   'Creating "Dangerous Memory": Challenge for Asian and Korean Femi-
            nist Theology', *Ecumenical Review* 47.1: 21-31.
1996   'Han', in Letty M. Russell and J. Shannon Clarkson (eds.), *Dictionary of
            Feminist Theologies* (Louisville: Westminster Press): 134-35.
Katoppo, Marianne
1979   *Compassion and Free: An Asian Woman's Theology* (Geneva: World Council
            of Churches).
Kim, Myong Hi
1992   'The Situation and Problem of Korean Women Ministers', *In God's Image*
            11.2: 10-18.
Kim, Yong Bock
1990   'The Mission of God in the Context of the Suffering and Struggling
            Peoples of Asia', in *Peoples of Asia, People of God: A Report of the Asian Mis-
            sion Conference, 1989* (Osaka: Christian Conference of Asia): 5-32.
King, Ursula (ed.)
1994   *Feminist Theology from the Third World* (London: SPCK).
Kinukawa, Hisako
1994   *Women and Jesus in Mark: A Japanese Feminist Perspective* (Maryknoll, NY:
            Orbis Books).
Kwak, Kyong Rang
1992   'Women Church of Korea', *In God's Image* 11.2: 8-9.
Kwok, Pui-lan
1984   'God Weeps with Our Pain', *East Asia Journal of Theology* 2.2: 228-32.
1992   *Chinese Women and Christianity, 1860–1927* (Atlanta: Scholars Press).
1993   'Chinese Non-Christian Perceptions of Christ', in Leonardo Boff and
            Virgil Elizondo (eds.), Concilium 1993/2 *Any Room for Christ in Asia?*
            (Maryknoll, NY: Orbis Books): 24-32.
1995a   'Business Ethics in the Economic Development of Asia: A Feminist Anal-
            ysis', *Asia Journal of Theology* 9.1: 133-45.
1995b   *Discovering the Bible in the Non-Biblical World* (Maryknoll, NY: Orbis Books).
1997   'Ecology and Christology', *Feminist Theology* 15: 113-25.
1998   'Jesus/the Native: Biblical Studies from a Postcolonial Perspective', in Fer-
            nando F.Segovia and Mary Ann Tolbert (eds.), *Teaching the Bible: The Dis-*

courses and Politics of Biblical Pedagogy (Maryknoll, NY: Orbis Books): 69-85.

Kwok, Pui-lan (ed.)

  1997   'Asian and Asian American Women's Voices', *Journal of Asian and Asian American Theology* 2.1: 1-139.

Lascano, Lydia L.

  1985   'Women and the Christ Event', in EATWOT 1985: 121-29.

  1985–86   'The Role of Women in the Church and in Society', *In God's Image* (December 1985-February 1986): 9-14.

Lee, Oo Chung

  1988   'Bible Study on Peace and Unification', *In God's Image* (June): 24-28.

  1994   *In Search for Our Foremothers' Spirituality* (Seoul: AWRC).

Lee, Oo Chung *et al.* (eds.)

  1992   *Women of Courage: Asian Women Reading the Bible* (Seoul: AWRC).

Lewis, Nantawan Boonprasat

  1986   'Asian Women Theology: A Historical and Theological Analysis', *East Asia Journal of Theology* 4.2: 18-22.

  1995   'Toward an Ethic of Feminist Liberation and Empowerment: A Case Study of Prostitution in Thailand', in Shin Chiba *et al.* (eds.), *Christian Ethics in Ecumenical Context* (Grand Rapids: Eerdmans): 219-30.

Lozada, Rebecca, and Alison O'Grady (eds.)

  1995   *Creation and Spirituality: Asian Women Expressing Christian Faith through Art* (Hong Kong: Christian Conference of Asia).

Mananzan, Mary John

  1988   'Who Is Jesus Christ?', *Voices from the Third World* 11.2: 1-16.

  1989   'Redefining Religious Commitment in the Philippine Context', in Fabella and Park (eds.): 101-14.

  1993   'Paschal Mystery from a Philippine Perspective', in Leonardo Boff and Virgil Elizondo (eds.), *Concilium* 1993/2: *Any Room for Christ in Asia?* (Maryknoll, NY: Orbis Books): 86-94.

Mananzan, Mary John (ed.)

  1991   *Essays on Women* (Manila: St. Scholastica's College, rev. edn, 1991).

  1992   *Women and Religion* (Manila: St. Scholastica's College, rev. edn, 1992).

Mananzan, Mary John *et al.* (eds.)

  1996   *Women Resisting Violence: Spirituality for Life* (Maryknoll, NY: Orbis Books).

Matsui, Yayori

  1989   *Women's Asia* (London: Zed Books).

Mies, Maria

  1986   *Patriarchy and Accumulation on a World Scale* (London: Zed Books).

Mies, Maria, and Vandara Shiva

  1993   *Ecofeminism* (London: Zed Books).

Ng, Ann

  1982   'On the Book of Ruth', *In God's Image* (December): 9-10.

Ng, Greer Ann Wenh-In

  1997   'Inclusive Language in Asian North American Churches: Non-Issue or Null Curriculum', *Journal of Asian and Asian American Theology* 2.1: 21-36.

Ong, Aihwa

  1987   *Spirits of Resistance and Capitalist Discipline: Factory Women in Malaysia* (New York: State University of New York Press).

Panikkar, Raimundo
    1987   'The Jordan, the Tiber and the Ganges', in John Hick and Paul F. Knitter (eds.), *The Myth of Christian Uniqueness: Toward a Pluralistic Theology of Religions* (Maryknoll, NY: Orbis Books): 89-116.

Park, Sun Ai Lee
    1987   'Understanding the Bible from Women's Perspective', *Voices from the Third World* 10.2: 66-75.
    1989   'Envisioning a Future Church as an Asian Woman', *Voices from the Third World* 12.1: 64-94.

Perera, Marlene
    1991   'Towards a New Humanity: Christianity and Buddhism in Dialogue', in AWRC: 207-10.

Porter, H.D.
    1890   'The Missionary Invasion of China', *Chinese Recorder* 21: 291-305.

Rebera, Ranjini
    1990   *A Search for Symbols: An Asian Experiment* (Manila: Christian Conference of Asia).
    1997   'Power and Equality', *In God's Image* 16.4: 44-49.

Ruether, Rosemary Radford
    1983   *Sexism and God-Talk: Toward a Feminist Theology* (Boston: Beacon Press).

Sanneh, Lamin
    1989   *Translating the Message: The Missionary Impact on Culture* (Maryknoll, NY: Orbis Books).

Schüssler Fiorenza, Elisabeth
    1984   *In Memory of Her: A Feminist Theological Reconstruction of Christian Origins* (New York: Crossroad).
    1994   *Jesus: Miriam's Child, Sophia's Prophet* (New York: Continuum).

Schüssler Fiorenza, Elisabeth (ed.)
    1993   *Searching the Scriptures. I. A Feminist Introduction* (New York: Crossroad).

Shiva, Vandara
    1989   *Staying Alive: Women, Ecology and Development* (London: Zed Books,).

Song, C.S.
    1982   *The Compassionate God* (Maryknoll, NY: Orbis Books).

Spivak, Gayatri Chakravorty
    1985   'Three Women's Texts and a Critique of Imperialism', *Critical Inquiry* 12: 243-61.
    1987   *In Other Words: Essays in Cultural Politics* (New York: Methuen).
    1990   *The Post-Colonial Critic: Interviews, Strategies, Dialogues* (New York: Routledge).

Suchocki, Majorie Hewitt
    1987   'In Search of Justice: Religious Pluralism from a Feminist Perspective', in John Hick and Paul F. Knitter (eds.), *The Myth of Christian Uniqueness*: 149-61.

Sugirtharajah, R.S.
    1998a   *Asian Biblical Hermeneutics and Postcolonialism: Contesting the Interpretations* (Maryknoll, NY: Orbis Books).
    1998b   'A Postcolonial Exploration of Collusion and Construction in Biblical

Interpretation', in R.S. Sugirtharajah (ed.), *The Postcolonial Bible* (Sheffield: Sheffield Academic Press): 91-116.

Tan, Yak Hwee
    1989   'Ecclesiology and Women', in Abraham *et al.* (eds.) 1989a: 273-77.

Tapia, Elizabeth S.
    1992   'Women in Solidarity with Women', *In God's Image* 11.4: 24-28.

Tauli-Corpuz, Victoria
    1996   'Reclaiming Earth-Based Spirituality: Indigenous Women in the Cordillera', in Rosemary Radford Ruether (ed.), *Women Healing Earth* (Maryknoll, NY: Orbis): 99-106.

Ten Percent Club
    1997   'Homosexual Declaration', *In God's Image* 16.3: 49.

Thein, Nyunt Nyunt
    1989   'Ecclesiology and Women' in Abraham *et al.* (eds.): 269-72.

Trinh, T. Minh-Ha
    1989   *Woman, Native, Other: Writing Postcoloniality and Feminism* (Bloomington: Indiana University Press).

Truong, Thanh-dam
    1990   *Sex, Money and Morality: Prostitution and Tourism in South-East Asia* (London: Zed Books).

Wang, Lily Kuo
    1989   'Ecclesiology and Women: A View from Taiwan', in Fabella and Park (eds.): 24-32.

Williams, Delores S.
    1991   'Black Women's Surrogacy Experience and the Christian Notion of Redemption', in Paula M. Cooey *et al.* (eds.), *After Patriarchy: Feminist Transformation of World Religions* (Maryknoll, NY: Orbis Books): 1-14.

Women's Concerns Unit, Christian Conference of Asia (ed.)
    1986   *Reading the Bible as Asian Women* (Singapore: Christian Conference of Asia).

Wong, Agatha Mei-yuk
    1989   'The Ministries of Women in Paul's Letter', in Abraham *et al.* (eds.) 1989a: 278-83.
    1997   'Women, Priesthood and Power', *In God's Image* 16.1: 13-16.

Wong, Angela Wai Ching
    1999   'Negotiating for a Postcolonial Identity: Christian Discourse on "The Poor Women" in Asia' (unpublished paper).

Yong, Ting Jin
    1989   'A Protestant Perspective', in Fabella and Park (eds.): 44-51.

Yuasa, Yuko
    1996   'Magdalene Dancing in Crimson: A Biblical Noh Drama', *Japan Christian Activity News* (Spring/Summer): 2-3.

Zambrano, Aurora
    1987   'Mariology', in Abraham *et al.* (eds.) 1989a: 222-27.

INDEXES

INDEX OF REFERENCES

BIBLE

INDEX OF AUTHORS